# TABLE OF C

# Acknowledgements

I want to thank the people that were a big part of this journey whether it was through emotional support, coaching, pushing me to face uncomfortable situations, or giving me the opportunity to be under the limelight.

Thank you to Jared for giving me a platform and introducing me to so many amazing people, Anna for supporting my growth and being there to help, Kosmo for being the source of energy and inspiration that has impacted so many lives, Stephen for being the genius businessman that he is, sharing his wealth of knowledge with me, and going the distance for me when he didn't have to, and Valentina for being my backbone through thick and thin. Lastly, special thanks to my dog Luna for keeping me company during the long nights of writing.

This book would not have been possible without everyone involved.

# About the Author

Gor was not a natural growing up. He was the socially awkward kid that never really fit in. He was the guy who laughed a beat too late at jokes, his attempts at small talk would fall short, and he couldn't take an interaction from start to finish even when a girl liked him.

He traveled across the world to pursue freedom and opportunity like many immigrant families and found himself in the midst of different cultures and traditions. Little did he know this would be the spark that would propel him to develop passions he never expected. Until then, he would deal with every obstacle there was in the social realm.

He was never the cool kid in school. He focused on his grades and could not keep relationships with people. He had pent up sexual shame, crippling social anxiety, and on top of that he would never talk in group settings or put himself out there under social pressure.

There came a day where he was sick and tired of being sick and tired and decided to never again allow his own limiting beliefs and low level emotions stop him from living a full life. He never wanted to be the guy on his deathbed regretting the life he could have had if he had only given himself permission to pursue the things he was passionate about. So, that's what he did.

Even though he was studying political science and business at the time, he was obsessed with learning cognitive behavioral psychology to understand why people do what they do and respond the way they respond to different things or even the same thing in different scenarios. He wanted to understand also how to influence these behaviors whether it be in changing his own habits or negotiating a business deal. It was fascinating to him how easily the human mind was influenced and he set out to learn and master communication in the form of building empathy, learning to listen, using NLP and hypnosis to be able to not only change his own habits, but help people change theirs.

He saw women as a mirror in his journey in developing himself and spent the following decade learning from books, coaches, and people in his circle that were naturally great with social skills and communication. This book is the introduction of what he learned in the field and what he has to share with you.

# Foreword

Gor is the personification of the introvert who somehow flips a switch and becomes the life of the party. Yeah, that guy. The one who seems to effortlessly mingle, making everyone feel like they've been friends for ages. And let's not skip over the fact that he's got this cool, approachable aura—tall, good-looking, and has this vibe that draws you in. People just love being around him.

Before I became the winner of the VH1 show "The Pickup Artist," I knew nothing about how to talk to women. For a long time I would just get by without really knowing the intricacies between men and women. It wasn't until I was pushed to my limits under my old mentor that I really grew. So, I wish I had a guide like this book back then because it took me several years of working on personal development to master this skill. This book is a goldmine of lessons on personal growth, wrapped up in a story that's as relatable as it is motivational.

I've seen Gor work with clients firsthand. He has coached men struggling who could not talk to women, who's conversations fell short and they couldn't lead to a date, and men who just had anxiety and could not even approach someone to begin with. I've seen their transformation after working with Gor and how unrecognizable they were. These are very few select people that he works with and you should consider it a blessing that you get a glimpse into his coaching.

I don't have any doubt that this book will go down as one of the textbook guides for social skills in the future. This will be a book that many other books will try to replicate.

Working with Gor will be the best decision for your future. Having watched Gor's own transformation up close, I can vouch for the magic that happens when someone dives deep into personal development. And that's exactly why I'm excited for you to dive into this book. It's not just another read; it's a tool that's going to transform how you see yourself and what you're capable of.

My advice? Share this book with others. It's the kind of act that does more than just spread good energy; it helps everyone around you level up with you. Gor's journey is a masterclass in breaking through limits and making significant strides in life, and this book is your ticket to getting in on that action.

So, as you flip through these pages, think of it as grabbing coffee with Gor, where he shares the ins and outs of turning introspection into outward success. It's a friendly chat that promises to shift how you approach your goals and life. Get ready for some real talk, some hearty laughs, and a ton of inspiration.

– Alvaro 'Kosmo' Manrique

Winner of VH1's "The Pickup Artist"

# Preface

In a world where the images of high value men are often painted with extravagance and machismo, it's crucial to take a step back and question what truly constitutes value. If you're expecting tips on how to channel your inner Andrew Tate and flash your way to the top, you might want to adjust those expectations. Let this book be a wake up call that it's not about the bling, the fancy rides, or living large. This book is about diving deeper, way past the surface stuff, to what really counts.

While there's no denying the appeal of material riches—and indeed, everyone wants material wealth and financial prosperity—these factors alone do not define a high value man. The essence of being truly valuable stems from deeper, more intangible qualities that resonate with who you are at your core, not just what you possess.

As I write this book, I am on my own lifelong journey of personal development with multiple coaches and mentors and always looking for more ways to develop myself and grow. When ESPN interviewed the great Michael Jordan in the last year of his career, they asked him why he was working with several coaches even though he was the greatest basketball player of all time. His response was that he was the best of the best BECAUSE he had those coaches.

This book is not an end all be all, but my desire is to be one of your many coaches in helping you discover what it means to be a high value man.

# Introduction: You Have it all Wrong

The question that's usually asked is "How do I get the girl?"

What do you think is wrong with that question?

The mindset.

Why? Because asking that question assumes that you need to DO a magic move and then walk away with the girl. Read that sentence again, we're going to dive deep into it later.

For now, here's a story about perspective.

I was having a conversation with one of my friends who was having sex with a bunch of different women. At the time I looked up to him for being able to pull so many women, but that day he told me he's tired of it. I thought "how can someone get tired of what we are made to do?" I didn't believe him, there had to be something more to the story.

He told me he felt empty sleeping around with a bunch of women and they never saw him for anything more than that. He would get attached and end up pushing them away. He built up a resentment towards them, but decided to do the opposite of what most guys would have done. Instead of feeding that dark energy and pursuing women even more just to use them for having mistreated him, he decided to drop the entire thing, get married and settle down with a religious girl and start a family. Although I'm not at all against marriage and starting a family, the perspective he had on women and what it means to be "successful" with women I did not agree with.

I always saw him as an abundant man, but that day my perspective on abundance shifted and I gained a new understanding of what it meant to be a high value man. Having seen scarcity with women, and not had much success before, he had learned to get good and gained an abundance of women around him. After our conversation, I realized there are different levels of abundance. What he had was an abundance of women and sex, but the next level of abundance is connection, and he was still lacking that.

As men, we often crave intimacy more than sex, and oftentimes, men get on this journey for the wrong reasons because we confuse that abundance and this leads us down a rabbit hole. The dangers of having "fake abundance" is that it will leave us questioning our self-worth because we didn't take the time to connect with people, and when we do, we end up pushing them away. This leads us down a rabbit hole of drowning self-worth and depressive thoughts because we start associating these results with our core identity.

My clients that have ended up making strides forward in their progress, experiencing epiphanies, and seeing results are the ones that asked "How do I BECOME the person that a girl is drawn to?"

The aim of this book is to pass along to you the right understanding of what being good with women truly means and get you in the right headspace to get there. If you follow everything covered in this book, you will have success with women in more ways than you thought possible.

Before you embark on this journey, you must first commit to the right perspective and understand that you are in it for yourself, not the girl.

Now we can get the show on the road.

# SECTION I

## MODELING THE HIGH VALUE MINDSET

# CHAPTER 1 | The Student Becomes the Master

*"Man cannot remake himself without suffering, for he is both the marble and the sculptor."*
*- Alexis Carrel*

I've spent over 10 years practicing this craft, and seeking out the right mentors to learn from.

I came to the United States from Armenia not knowing anyone. When I went to school I didn't know English and there was a big cultural difference between me and all the other kids so I had trouble relating. I had trouble fitting in and I spent all of my elementary school years trying to learn and understand the language. I would read books, watch TV shows, and stay after class to assimilate.

In middle school I had finally transferred to regular English classes and kept my head in my books. I wouldn't socialize much with the other kids at this point in my life. I was part of several clubs at school, one of which was the Junior Ambassadors club where we would pick up trash on campus and do beach cleanups. Maybe those values were instilled in me because I still don't like littering, and keeping my environment clean is a big deal to me.

Anyway, I would basically spend my lunch time in the classroom where we would have our club meetings with other students that were part of the organization. I was also a teacher's pet. On holidays I would take my teachers gifts and keep good relations with them. I even had good relationships with the principal and assistant principal and the office staff. One time I had In-N-Out for lunch with the assistant principal.

At home I would spend the entirety of my days doing homework and studying and had a straight 'A' average all of middle school. I got the president's academic award at graduation. In reality my homework could have taken me an hour or two to finish, but I would put pressure on myself and feel guilty for not working and extend that time to finish homework longer than it should have taken me. I still struggle with that to this day even though I've gotten better at managing it.

In high school I tried to be one of the cool kids. All that happened was that my GPA went down, I got a crush on a girl who convinced me to change schools with her, and I wasn't even invited to senior "ditch day" when everyone was skipping school. In high school, I would watch the sunset from my Calculus class countless times. I was still a favorite student in a lot of my classes. I had a few friends that I would hang out with at lunch in the same place every day and just wait for lunch to be over so we can go back to class and go home.

I had female friends, and I even had some girls that liked me, but I was completely unaware of it at the time. Even if I had noticed, I wouldn't know what to do with it or where to take it.

Coming from a very traditional background, I had a lot of sexual shame and performance guilt. I got the typical "Study hard because we sacrificed a lot for you," "Get a job, get married, have kids," and "Stay out of trouble, come home early, you don't need to be out every day." Even on summer vacation, I would stay home and watch Disney channel most of the day if I wasn't taking a class to get ahead.

It's safe to say I've never been a popular kid, and I didn't get to experience much of life and make my own mistakes throughout my childhood. I can't blame anyone, my parents kept me safe and have saved my life multiple times. They always steered me in the right direction and growing up sheltered was just part of that. As an adult the rest is my responsibility.

Around college time I started taking interest in developing my social skills because I was tired of the way my personality was and I didn't know that it was a learnable skill. I remember the first time I searched on YouTube "how to talk to girls." I still think back to that and laugh about where I started.

I started working on my skills, allowing myself to approach women and talk to them and trying to be more open with strangers in general. Even though I lived on campus and made friends with classmates, I spent most of my time with my roommates. I was the ultimate introvert, to the extent that I went downtown only once throughout the entire time I was in college. I didn't have a car and I didn't get out much. I went to University of California San Diego, and to my luck, it wasn't really a party college, we didn't even have frat houses. I remember my coworkers would make fun of me at the time I was getting ready to go to college, saying I'm going to start getting out of my shell and drinking. Turns out that was San Diego State University. That was party central, people from our school would go there to party.

The one time in college I accidentally got invited on a party bus was when my roommate and I were trying to throw a party at our suite and we went around inviting half the building. We knocked on one door and a girl opened. We told her and her roommate that we're throwing a party and they instead invited us on their party bus that was going to some club and they were leaving in an hour. I thought this was my chance to meet cool people and do something fun for once. I went and changed quickly and went on the party bus. At the club, the girl that invited me came to dance with me and she was asking how my night was going, making conversation, and she turned to grind on me. I was super shy and didn't know what to do, but I caught feelings thinking she must like me and I like her too. After we danced, she went to mingle and I saw her making out with a guy from the party bus that she ended up taking home. The entire ride home I watched them flirt and kiss, and the couple next to me saw how sad I looked and brought me into their conversation.

All the moments in my life that have helped me open up, have had to do with someone offering a safe space to express myself. This couple spent the whole ride including me in their conversation and I went home in a better mood, but still contemplating what I'm doing wrong. I wasn't really doing anything to begin with, but I didn't see that.

I don't say all this for sympathy, I say to prove a point that if I was able to do it so can you.

My journey was long and difficult. You might have guessed already, I was a late bloomer and even though I had some opportunities in college, something always seemed to happen that gave me an excuse to chicken out. I would get anxious and make excuses, and so I ended up losing my virginity at 23 years old. From then on, I went on a rampage with dating and learning.

I realized part of what was motivating me was the resentment that came from years of what I thought was rejection, but I was the one doing the wrong things and not understanding why I got responses that I interpreted as hurtful at the time even though not all of them were.

I started dating 3 girls at once, keeping my options open, never committing to anyone, going from girl to girl. I started approaching more, learning what to say, and practicing. I signed up for all the online dating apps on the side and went on dates through there as well. I was on a mission.

I reached a point where I had an abundance of women, but I felt alone. It was becoming a routine to do the same things, say the same things, and go to the same places. I started questioning if that was all there was to dating and connecting. I refused to accept that people could be narrowed down to a simple system of interaction and have no human component. Systems are necessary for everything, but at most as a foundation and not the basis for an entire connection with someone. I was going down a rabbit hole feeling more empty with every new girl as it began to lose meaning after a while.

I realized two things from that phase in my life. One was that the feeling of loneliness is a need for validation and getting validation is only a bandaid on the wound, not the solution. At its core, loneliness is a state of mind. Two different people can be in the same situation and one can feel lonely and the other not at all. Again, that ended up pointing the cause of my issues back towards me. What was I missing that wasn't allowing me to connect? It was me that wasn't allowing myself to feel vulnerable, to be open to connection, and talking about myself more. I grew up with a "tough love" mentality to which emotions were not only secondary, but a weakness. I started seeing patterns of girls telling me that they don't know anything about me, or asking me questions about me saying I haven't shared anything about myself. I noticed I had an innate resistance to opening up that I was not even aware of that wasn't allowing me to connect with people because I didn't feel safe.

Hence, the other thing I realized was that an abundance of women does not mean an abundance of connection. I was dating a lot, but I did not allow myself to connect with people. I was still reserved and focused on the other person more than myself. Slowly I began to track down the causes of all the things I wasn't happy with back to myself. I didn't want to connect because I was afraid to, and I came off emotionally unavailable and as a byproduct attracted the toxic people those traits spoke to most.

I learned late that we all need to work on ourselves and the world is really lacking emotional intelligence and empathy. My own journey taught me what many men go through in their development and that most of them stop because it gets too frustrating and they don't have the proper guidance to steer them in the right direction. I knew I had no alternative because I was not willing to stay the same, and it ended up working out for me because I committed myself to things that I could not get out of when things got hard.

I was reading books on influence, negotiation, body language, emotional intelligence, mental health, and shadow work. I started hiring coaches to teach me more about myself. I realized this has been more than just a journey to not feel alone. Feeling alone was never the problem.

One of my mentors took me under his wing and spent a year teaching me because at the time I could not afford it, but I was doing everything I could to work on myself. I spent a year with him learning and helping him teach others until I started teaching people on my own.

I started treating women as human beings because I understood them so much better. All the things that men consider stupid or irrational that women do, I suddenly agreed with. I got many female friends, which gave me an even bigger glimpse into their world and what they go through. I realized there is no such thing as the "friendzone." I choose to actually be friends with all of my female friends, but there is still the understanding of that man to woman dynamic. There is still sexual tension and playful flirting but it comes from a different place and with different intentions. That is the only difference. I prefer to be friends with a woman first to better get to know her and see where she fits in my life. I don't like to rush into things or lead people on. I still didn't want a relationship and all the girls I was involved with knew that. I had a different appreciation for that feminine energy, it was no longer all about sex.

I was getting invited out to events and meeting more people. I started doing events too and inviting a bunch of my female friends. I was the guy who always had girls around him and my friends would make comments like "I live through your instagram stories."

When I was starting out, if you had told me I would be teaching people how to understand, empathize, and communicate with women while growing to become the best versions of themselves, I would never have believed you. I ended up here because my passions brought me here, and I deeply needed to understand myself. I was blessed to have encountered the people who got me to this point, and now I know that the world needs this. Most of the suffering and low level emotions present in the world such as shame, hate, and anger stem from internal states that people often do not take the time to understand because it's easier to complain and blame others first.

I started off as reserved, dorky, insecure, and clueless as it gets. Now I teach this. You can absolutely have the girl of your dreams. It's reachable, but you won't see the big picture during your journey, you can only see where you are when you get there and look back on how far you've come.

# CHAPTER 2 | The Daytime Connection Game - Why It's a Big Deal

*"And as we let our own light shine, we unconsciously give other people permission to do the same. As we are liberated from our fear, our presence automatically liberates others."*
**- Marianne Williamson**

Alright, let's dive into something that often gets overlooked but is an absolute game-changer - making connections with people during the day. Trust me, this isn't just small talk; it's a life skill that can seriously level up your game in personal development and relationships. When you connect with people during the day, it no longer becomes about making time to "go out and socialize," this is your life, you're already living it, going about your day. If that wasn't reason enough to learn the skill, let's dive into why it's crucial for you to learn.

## Seizing Everyday Moments

Consider the canvas of your daily life - the moments you spend waiting for your coffee, grabbing a quick lunch, or navigating through your workplace. These seemingly routine instances hold immense potential for connection. Unlike the orchestrated scenes of a night out, daytime interactions are like discovering hidden gems in the fabric of the everyday. They offer a unique opportunity to turn the mundane into the extraordinary, providing a fresh perspective on life by finding meaningful connections in unexpected places. Seizing these everyday moments becomes a practice of recognizing and embracing the beauty in the ordinary. It's about cultivating a heightened awareness of the present, transforming seemingly mundane moments into opportunities for connection, and appreciating the richness of life in its simple, unscripted moments.

Lifestyle isn't about how lavish your experiences are, it's about how you show up on the day to day and what you bring to the table. You can go spend $30,000 at a club and be depressed and you can go grocery shopping and have the best time. It starts with your mental state, and how your day ends and your next day begins and every moment in between.

## Becoming a Social Wizard

This is my all time favorite reason because it's a literal super power. Daytime connections are not just about mastering casual chit-chat; they serve as a transformative journey toward becoming a social wizard. It's an immersive learning experience where you pick up the subtle nuances of social dynamics. From deciphering unspoken cues to reading body language like a seasoned pro, these daytime encounters become your training ground.

The skills acquired extend beyond charming someone at a café; they empower you to navigate the complex landscape of professional networking, excel in social gatherings, and form meaningful connections in personal relationships. Imagine walking out of every social situation leaving people craving your presence and wanting you to be a part of their social circle and introduce you to others.

It's not just about being socially adept; it's about mastering the intricate dance of human interaction. As you evolve into a social wizard, you find yourself not just navigating conversations but orchestrating them, creating harmonies that resonate across various aspects of your life. You will see through people, their intentions, their feelings, their traumas, their rationale, and even certain things they have going on in their life based on the patterns you catch in person. It's like seeing the matrix while everyone else is simply a part of it.

## Facing the Fear of Saying "Hi"

Approaching someone in broad daylight demands a unique kind of courage. Unlike the comforting cloak of darkness, the daytime requires you to boldly own your confidence. This means walking in with conviction and thoughts in your mind saying "Fuck yeah, it's me, I'm interrupting you." If you dig into this thought process, you'll see that there is a lot going on in the back end. First, you're owning the fact that you're walking up to her, and then you're owning the fact that you might be interrupting her day or causing some inconvenience in the moment.

Most guys reject themselves before they get a chance to be rejected. Oftentimes you perceive that you're causing an inconvenience. She might even be happy to be getting approached, but the thoughts in your head are telling you you're not welcome. If that's the case, that's where the mindset comes in... It's ok that you're not welcome; it's ok that you're interrupting her day. That's what you tell yourself. There are levels to mindset, and that was the first level.

If you are a level above that then you know that you're adding value to her day by approaching her and she might be the one that reacts badly. In that instance you would tell yourself that you did something wrong and that's ok, it's just practice and you did well for putting yourself out there.

Then the highest level of this mindset is the ultimate high value abundance mentality. Not only are you owning the fact that you are approaching her and could potentially be interrupting her day whether you know it or not and that's ok, but you're also not thrown off by any reaction. You expect a good reaction because that's how the world has treated you so that's what you're used to. Therefore, the high value man doesn't think he got rejected because rejection is a made-up concept. If the Chooser gets a bad reaction, he doesn't think he got rejected, he instead turns to empathy and feels bad for the girl because she must be having a bad day.

This isn't to say that you go do something clearly stupid or aggressive and blame the girl for it. Do not misunderstand me, because along with the mindset you must develop the skills that come from having high emotional intelligence. Therefore, knowing that he did nothing wrong, the Chooser is unphased by any negative reaction because he is not only aware of himself but also aware of the emotional state of others.

Not to get too deep on this topic now, but that just goes to show what I was saying earlier about seeing the matrix. There is so much that goes into saying a simple "hi" from the current internal emotional state, to the mental state, to the external acts and ways in which they are executed and what that says about you.

Mastering the seemingly simple act of saying "hi" becomes a powerful tool, transcending its role in romantic pursuits. It's a catalyst for an overall boost in self-confidence, a fearless embrace of your social prowess that transcends time and setting. Daytime interactions become a canvas for cultivating a sense of fearlessness in any social situation, whether in the vibrant light of day or the mysterious allure of the night. This newfound courage extends beyond mere greetings; it becomes a mindset that propels you to face challenges head-on, transforming fear into an opportunity for growth and self-discovery.

## Mixing It Up with Different Crowds

You know you've made it into the top 1% of men in the world when you're able to mix and be a part of different crowds without being fake or changing yourself to please others. Daytime connections act as gateways to these diverse social circles. Imagine having the power to find a communication style to be able to speak and relate to people from all different walks of life. It's like injecting a burst of fresh perspectives and untapped opportunities into your social landscape, and the more you're able to connect with different people the more you will be able to connect with different people. It's a self-fulfilling prophecy, but you must first get to the level of being able to understand and relate to diverse groups of people. One of the most beautiful aspects is the empathy that grows within you. As you listen to others' stories, challenges, and victories, you start to feel the world through their eyes.

By mingling with different crowds during the day, you open yourself up to a richer tapestry of relationships. It's an invitation to step out of your comfort zone, embrace variety, and experience the world through the lens of diverse perspectives. The more you diversify your social circles, the more you enrich your life with a kaleidoscope of experiences, fostering a deeper understanding of the human tapestry.

Imagine having conversations that go beyond the surface, where you connect with someone on a level that transcends cultural boundaries. Learning to communicate effectively with people from different walks of life opens your eyes to the beauty of our shared humanity. The most beautiful experiences I've had in life have revolved around people and being introduced to new worlds that they hold. I'll go into the stories later in this chapter.

## Real Talk, Real Connections

Not only is meeting people during your day-to-day a way of life, but peeling away the layers of fancy nighttime ambiance and social masks; daytime connections thrive on authenticity. Whether you find yourself discussing shared hobbies with a coworker or engaging in animated conversations about art in a museum, the authenticity of these interactions forms the foundation for meaningful connections.

No more superficial small talk; it's time for real, raw conversations. Daytime becomes a stage for sharing genuine moments, fostering connections that go beyond surface-level interactions, and creating relationships that stand the test of authenticity. As you engage in real talk, you not only deepen your connections but also create a space for vulnerability and honesty, fostering a sense of trust that transcends the superficial.

## Connecting With Yourself

The whole reason I got into mastering this skill with women, is because I realized that other people are a direct mirror into your deeper self. I later proved this to myself with something I was aware of at the time in myself - I was very judgmental. As I learned to be open-minded and judge people less, or even waste energy on considering judging them, I learned that I too felt less judged by others. The moment I became aware of this, it blew my mind. It was such a big epiphany that I remember the moment I felt it. I was walking outside the cafeteria building of my high school going to the other side of the building where my classes were and thinking about something feeling different that day. I would always have a fear of being judged or looking stupid, but that day I wasn't feeling that way and I had been working on judging people less. Then it came to me, I myself did not feel judged anymore.

Later on I started meeting people of the same mind. I remember an instance not too long after with this girl who was sober, but dancing like she was in her own room. She was living in joy and authenticity. I asked her, "what makes you so free?" She told me "the people that judge your freedom, are the ones that crave it the most," and I never forgot that.

Your interactions become more than just opportunities to make connections; they transform into moments of deep, meaningful connection. It's a journey into the heart of mindfulness, where every encounter becomes a chance to understand yourself and others on a more profound level.

Daytime connections become a portal to a richer, more intentional way of living. As you embrace mindful connections, you not only enhance the quality of your interactions but also cultivate a sense of gratitude for the present moment, enriching your life with a profound sense of purpose and connection.

In summary, mastering the art of daytime connections is not merely a social hack; it's a profound life upgrade. From refining your social skills to broadening your social circle, the benefits permeate every nook and cranny of your personal and professional life. So, why wait? Embrace the vibrancy of daytime interactions, explore the richness embedded in everyday moments, and get ready for a life that is more connected, fulfilling, and authentically yours.

You never know who you're going to meet.

I have so many stories of beautiful experiences and they have all revolved around people, spontaneity, and being open to connection.

You meet people that connect you in business, expand your social circle, or open your eyes to brand new life experiences and perspectives.

I was running a bootcamp in New York once and I stopped to see one of my students talking to two girls sitting across from each other having coffee. By the time I got to him, my other student had joined to help out with conversation. I thought nothing of it and hung around for a bit to listen and give them feedback afterwards but the conversation kept going.

Eventually, the one that had started the conversation ended up dropping the ball, and I thought the conversation was going to be over. To my surprise, the other student kept it going. As the first student left to join back the group of students, I thought this was a great learning opportunity for the second student that was keeping conversation going so I found an opening to transition into the conversation and keep my student in it.

I won't get too deep into the techniques, but my student, and I were in sync enough to communicate, and understand each other without saying anything. He understood my body language, and I was able to coach him within the conversation in order to move the conversation forward. We had built enough rapport with the girls to sit down with them, and I got the message across to him to pull himself a chair and close the distance with the girl that he was talking to, and isolate her attention so that it's more focused on him based on his positioning while I did something similar with the other girl. There were several points where I thought the conversation was going to be over, and my student was going to drop the ball, but I was so proud of him knowing when to pick up on cues to not only keep the conversation going, but to move it forward.

I coached him through some escalation tactics during the interaction as the four of us were talking and demonstrated a few myself. We ended up exchanging contact information with the girls and joining back with the rest of the students. During the interaction I had tested several forms of compliance with the girl that I was talking to, and I was breaking that down to my student. One of the things I tested for was bringing up the topic of dancing together. At the time, she was not invested enough to follow through with the compliance test and the key there was that I was calibrated enough to not push for it and redirected the conversation. A lot of times your level of emotional intelligence will be evident not by the things you do but by the things you refrain from doing. Most guys would have pushed to get up and dance because they're not used to handling rejection, but how you handle a "no" says a lot to the girl.

Later that night, those two girls had gone to a high end club in Manhattan because they had a friend who was a promoter and he had offered them a free table and bottle service since they were visiting from Europe. To no surprise, I got a text message from the girl that I was talking to earlier that day inviting me to join her and her friend at the table.

Here's a quick lesson for the more advanced men that are able to get to this point in an interaction where you get invited to events. Whenever you come across a situation where you are not the host at an event, you must still maintain your frame as a leader. Now, if I had to join them at the table and just sit there and drink, I guarantee they would not enjoy it and that night wouldn't last very long. When a girl initiates an interaction, that does not mean that you can be a passive participant. As a Chooser, you are still the leader of your environment, even if you are leading towards someone else's destination.

In this case, it was their table and their event that they were inviting me to and I was simply joining them. Instead of going there and asking them what we're doing, I went there and took over the environment. Reading their signals, and noticing when they were tired or when they needed a break, I led them outside and back inside. Noticing moments of boredom, I spiked the excitement by changing the vibe and doing something different.

The moment I got there, I started making friends. By the end of the night I had made friends with the promoter, the security, and the 10 girls around us at the other table. I got us another free bottle from a different promoter there and started a limbo in the middle of the club, brought everybody into it and left with the girls.

Not only are these skills useful for having fun experiences, but they also open doors for you into new opportunities.

One of my closest friends is a girl I met during the day when she was going home from her yoga class. It turned out that she was a Miss Europe Universe contestant who ended up winning and I was there at her show, which she really appreciated. So, not only did we end up doing events together where I invited a dozen of my other female friends and had everyone sing happy birthday to my puppy who was turning 4, but because she was in the Hollywood scene and hung out with a lot of celebrities, I had a chance to meet one of my favorite celebrities from the famous movie Borat who ended up inviting me to dinner with him.

I've also flown around the country and met several business connects through this skill of connecting with people, one of whom is planning to beat the world record for the highest skydive, and another one ended up becoming my business mentor and helped grow my business tenfold, but I won't bore you with the details.

My point is first of all that this is not just about girls, and second of all, that you are missing out on so much in life by denying yourself the opportunity to grow and develop your emotional intelligence just because it takes work and you haven't had luck in the past.

Most people live their entire lives never once having approached a stranger outside, but there is so much beauty you're missing out on. People are falling into depression and don't understand why, but what they are not aware of is that they spend every day of their lives rejecting themselves. The thoughts running through your mind are the most crucial aspect of your life and is of utmost priority in your development. Not only that but also learning to manage your emotions from always being in survival and fight-or-flight mode, to being in a good mood, feeling empowered, and expecting the best in people. No, this is not bullshit hype. Yes, it is possible. Yes it is doable.

# CHAPTER 3 | 15 Lies About Success with Women

*"It is not the critic who counts; not the man who points out how the strong man stumbles, or where the doer of deeds could have done them better. The credit belongs to the man who is actually in the arena."*
**- Theodore Roosevelt**

We all have limiting beliefs whether it's about not being good enough or being so good that we don't deserve it. What differentiates winners and losers at the end of the day isn't that winners don't have these thoughts of doubt and fear, it's not that they don't come up with excuses, because excuses are often valid reasons. The difference between winners and losers is that they act, and they act in spite of the doubt, fear, and excuses by trusting the process and outworking those emotions.

When your mind sees that you are headed in a certain direction despite all its efforts to hold you back, to keep you the same, to stay comfortable, then it realizes that holding you back is no longer the thing that is helping your survival because you're too deep into the thing you're doing and there's no going back. So what happens? Your mind magically shifts to support what you are doing, but as long as you have an exit plan and you have one foot in and one foot out, it's not going to work, you will not change. You will keep operating under the same beliefs that got you to the place you don't want to be.

If your beliefs don't help you get to where you want to be, you need to condition new beliefs and get rid of the old ones. These are some of the most common lies people believe about themselves that hinder them from growing.

## 1. The "It's all about looks" Myth

Don't get me wrong, looks do matter no matter what any guru tells you, but you don't have to be the best looking in the room. You do have to look your best, however. A girl likes a clean guy who takes care of himself and how he presents himself over the hottest guy in the world who smells.

There's one thing I want to understand deeply to your core in regards to looks. If you don't internalize anything else in this section I want you to internalize this one line because even more than the tailored clothing, fresh haircut, and nice cologne it's more important that you like the way you look.

Have you ever noticed that when you have a brand new favorite shirt you seem to get complimented on it more than usual even though it's not any unique article of clothing? Even more, have you noticed that all the pieces of clothing you love to wear, you get complimented on more than the others even though the others don't look bad? Even more than that, I've had instances where girls would pick out my outfit, or a stylist friend would put something together for me and I would even get unfitted clothes tailored and none of them would get complimented the way my "Amsterdam" shirt gets complimented when I go to a cafe on random Wednesday to grab coffee. Why is this?

On the other hand, have you noticed that when you get bored of that favorite shirt, the compliments also stop coming? The shirt didn't change, you didn't rip it or ruin it in any way, but people somehow just stopped noticing as much. It's because people don't pick up on what the shirt looks like as much as they pick up on your energy. Therefore, this is to say that girls don't care as much about how you look, as they do about how you feel about the way you look.

Let that sink in.

## 2. The "It's all about money" Myth

I hear this so much especially from younger people that see everything on social media and jump to conclusions about what it takes to be good with women. They see men flaunting money, "making it rain" at the club, and singing about buying women everything they want. If you had to take a guess, would you say that those men are in happy and healthy relationships with emotionally healthy women? It would be highly unlikely. Men who use their wealth as the only means of having women around them are bound to be taken advantage of. Even if they do end up in a relationship, they will not understand how to meet the woman's needs and develop a disconnect between them. The women that are typically around these types of men typically have family issues and rely on their looks to get by. They have a false sense of reality and have developed a huge need for validation that will end up throwing them into an identity crisis later in life when they become old news. You will find a lot of these women complaining that it's hard to find a husband and settle down as they get older and come out of their prime.

The point is it's not all about money. Even if you had the money you would not want to make it about the money. Your real measure of skill is how much you're able to give the woman without any real world things.The more material the woman needs in the relationship, the less of her needs you are meeting emotionally.

When a girl ditches a guy wanting to pick her up in his Ferrari for a fancy dinner to go grab coffee with you, it's a different type of confidence boost. At that point you know you have something of value to offer her that she can't get from anywhere else, and that value is in who you are. Keep that in mind for later chapters when we talk about how change happens at an identity level.

Having said that, I'm not going to lie and say money does not matter at all. Yes, you don't have to be rich and you don't have to have material wealth. However, just like looks, money does matter to some extent and it does make a difference. BUT, again, you don't have to be the richest or have a lot of money, but you have to have the ambition and potential to get it. What does this mean? It means you can get a girl even if you're broke. Instead of trying to impress a girl by buying things you can't afford, you can show her that you are goal-oriented and have a plan to achieve them. Women value your inner potential and vision more than your material wealth.

## 3. The "You will suddenly meet the one" Myth

That's a limiting belief stemming out of insecurity as an excuse to not pursue what you want and put yourself out there.

There's a reason the divorce rate in the United States is nearly 50%. It's people who believe the person they meet is the person they were meant to be with. They never took the time to experience different things and people and develop their emotional intelligence to be able to at least identify patterns of behavior and get better at communication to better handle relationships.

The majority of people follow the crowd. They go about their lives and date whoever they end up with. Not many take initiative to go for exactly what they want. Even worse, not having the emotional intelligence to recognize and differentiate emotionally healthy behaviors with unhealthy ones leaves people in self-destructive long term relationships.

The divorce rate for people who have been married once before is even higher, at over 60%. These same people keep trying and repeating the same patterns with the same types of people because they themselves refuse to change or are not aware enough to change.

The fact that you've picked up this book means that you don't want to be part of that majority and settle for average.

My friends tell me "I live vicariously through you, the crazy things you do always with girls." I've even gotten "I'm your number 1 fan" from people who I had been friends with since before developing my skills to this level. If a relationship comes out of any connection you have with someone it should happen on your terms in the most natural way possible, not because you're afraid to lose the person, or because the girl is pushing for a relationship and you go along with it.

## 4. The "I'm too busy to meet people" Myth

I used to think this way until one of my mentors gave me a new perspective. You must understand that you will always be busy. It's not a matter of not having time, it's about what is valuable to you and what you choose to make time for. When you decide that you have time for the things that will benefit you in life such as your personal growth and relationships, you will be pleasantly surprised at how you're able to do both. You must decide that your growth and happiness is a priority.

## 5. The "I'm the prize" Myth

There is a lot of misinformation on the internet. People read somewhere or watch a video telling them to act like the prize in order to have confidence and they take it at full value. Whether you are the prize or not, she doesn't know that, so it counts for nothing.

If you are generally a high value guy but she does not value any of the things that make you high value, you do not have value with her. You can be a quarterback in the NFL, but if she thinks football is stupid and is obsessed with World of Warcraft, then someone who knows a lot about World of Warcraft and can show her something new and take her to exclusive gaming events to show some form of status in the field, then she is going to be higher value in her eyes than Tom Brady.

If you're a division 1 athlete but she has dreamed of becoming a chess champion all her life, she will be more impressed by your accomplishments in chess than in soccer.

Notice how in every one of these examples, accomplishments and status are a big part of where your value comes from. It's not just about playing the sport that she values, it's about having accomplishments in it. If she likes soccer players and you were on the junior varsity team in high school keeping the bench warm, she is not going to be impressed. I bring up sports examples because these are most straightforward and easy to understand.

Now, on the other hand, if she loves soccer players and you are a division 1 soccer player, you cannot expect her to fall head over heels for you if you don't know how to present yourself. Humility is a valuable quality. If you brag about all of your accomplishments it's a turnoff. If you don't mention them at all, she will never know. You must know how to show your personality without coming off as trying to impress her. In either case, the burden of conversation is on you in the beginning and it's your responsibility to show her that you are the prize, otherwise you won't be.

## 6. The "I learn it myself" Myth

Refusing to learn from others who have achieved what you are trying to achieve will exponentially prolong your journey from getting to where you want it to go and you will never reach your full potential alone.

You can read all the books, watch all the videos, and even go out and practice all you want, but if you're doing it wrong, you will learn the wrong thing and never understand why you are not getting the results you want. I've had clients that have done thousands of approaches before getting coaching, and all they did was learn to approach. They didn't know how to lead a full interaction forward, they didn't know how to show intention, and they didn't understand why they weren't building attraction and doing it in a way that is repeatable.

Having a coach will not only help you become aware of things you've been doing wrong, but it will also help you learn the most efficient way to not only get to but repeat the results you want to reach.

Why would you do it yourself and face the daily frustrations or figuring it out yourself, wasting time, when someone has already established a proven way of doing what you're trying to do. Why would you waste your time?

It was the biggest mistake of my life, save yourself the headache. I was working out for 2 years before I got real results because I finally got a mentor. I was doing business for a year, not making money, until I spent the little money I had to pay for a mentor, then I literally doubled my income in the following months.

Learn from people who've done it before.

## 7. The "I can't date until I'm the best version of myself" Myth

This is an internal trauma that comes from the belief that you're not good enough and you must reach a certain point until you are enough for someone. When you find your true love, you will continue to grow together, and that's what a partnership is meant to be.

Dating is part of the process of becoming the best version of yourself. You mature emotionally from every relationship you are in and learn more about yourself. Again, it is massively important to have mentors whether you are in a relationship or not because it is easy to fall into traps with the wrong people and end up in toxic relationships without being aware.

## 8. The "I'm already good with girls" Myth

Usually, the people thinking this are people who are either being used for their wealth or relying on online dating.

Lack of awareness with how you come off to girls can end up backfiring on you. It's not just about getting the results, it's more about earning them, mastering the process.

Others who believe this are typically the type that are attractive and are able to have relationships with girls that like them, but they are afraid to challenge themselves and typically end up with girls that like them more than they like the girl.

## 9. The "It's not cool to learn to talk to girls" Myth

It's not cool to go to the gym with a bunch of guys and watch each other bend over and squat up and down, but because it's mainstream and people understand its purpose, it has become cool. Even now, people might still make fun of someone starting their fitness journey because he might look silly trying and failing, but he keeps showing up. People judge to the level of their understanding, and judgment is irrelevant from people who don't understand or are not on your level.

In general, starting from the bottom has never been cool, and most people don't understand the journey as with all difficult things. It's only when people see you getting results that they start praising you and asking for advice.

## 10.The "Women don't want to be approached" Myth

Women dream about being approached on a random Wednesday at the grocery store. They want to meet someone. This is a common complaint among my female friends. So, it's not that they don't want to be approached, it's that they don't want to be approached by unaware, aggressive guys wanting something from them.

This is a major issue in society. Men won't know what they're doing, they'll gain the courage to approach a woman, say the wrong things and be punished for it. Women on the other hand, not knowing what the guy went through to approach her, only see that he is wanting something from them and feel threatened and want to leave. Then, feeling rejected and misunderstood, the guy develops a sense of resentment towards all women. Feeling defeated, he stops approaching as much, then women complain that men don't approach them, and the man thinks they're stupid for not understanding. In reality it's a vicious cycle of miscommunication with the guy not having the emotional awareness to communicate with a woman and understand her and the woman not having the awareness to empathize. Each party does only what they know, and what they know leads to a divide in society.

## 11. The "Women love a mysterious man" Myth

Contrary to popular belief, women you've never met are not going to be impressed by your mysterious behavior. Quite the opposite, if they are not suspicious or indifferent to it, they will assume that you have a shallow personality and there's not much to know about you. If you do end up attracting someone, it will be the wrong type of person who is operating in their traumas and craves the anxiety that comes from being ignored without realizing it.

In general, the cool guy never wins, especially when you put him up against someone that knows what he's doing and what value to offer a girl. James Bond was cool to the people that knew him because he was good at what he did, but if he went up to a stranger at the bar, his charm and elegance might cause some intrigue and curiosity, but it won't allow him to establish connections with people, keep female friends, and have a relationship. At most he will have a one night stand here and there with a girl who gets excited for that mystery, but that stuff gets old.

## 12.The "Women don't like nice guys, they like bad boys" Myth

It's not about being a nice guy, it's about not having the qualities women look for in a man such as confidence, standards, and communication skills. The nice guy is usually nice because that's all he can do. These types of guys are usually overly agreeable, and go with everything the girl wants as opposed to having their own opinions and boundaries.

What women are attracted to in a bad boy is not that he is an asshole to them, contrary to popular belief. Oftentimes the bad-boy persona comes with a sense of independence and self-assurance that a nice guy does not present. Women don't like an asshole, they like a man who is independent, confident in himself, and a leader of his own domain. That means he pursues what he wants without the permission or approval of others, and has values that are more important to him than any woman and must be respected.

A man must always move with a deliberate sense of purpose. That is the first thing a girl will notice about any guy is his demeanor and the way he carries himself in the world.

## 13.The "I'm too introverted to socialize" Myth

Yes, being introverted makes you want to isolate yourself from everybody and just be in your own world. Having this personality might make you feel like you will never socialize and meet people because you just don't have it in you. Here's some good news, I am an introvert.

Here's more good news. Not only is extroversion learnable and usable on command, but you can sway your behavior to lean one way or the other. For those that want to learn, it's very doable. You can test it by the Myers Briggs test and track how your personality adapts as you develop.

At the end of the day, the goal is to have that extroverted personality to bring out whenever you need it. Whether you're an extrovert or an introvert, developing a captivating personality and knowing how to work a room and influence others takes time and effort to learn.

## 14.The "It costs too much to hire a coach" Myth

After witnessing so many horror stories in my time as a coach, I can tell you - it costs too much not to.

Would it be cheaper to settle down with someone, grow old and lose everything you have in a divorce settlement, or to put the work in early on and choose a partner out of abundance instead of societal pressure or lack of options? Not only did you lose half your assets, but more importantly you lost time. Money is something you can always get back, but you can never bring back time and to get a second chance.

Live your life as if this is your second chance, and prioritize yourself over money. When you determine that you are more important than your material wealth, the material wealth will naturally follow, because you will grow to the level of achieving it.

## 15.The "It's cool to be a player" Myth

Oftentimes, the people who think this way lack empathy. Leading a girl on for the sake of getting something from her and then breaking her heart is not cool. Girls sometimes do this as well, and it is a sign of immaturity.

No girl likes a player. A player is someone who plays women for his own benefit. Most guys think that being a player is cool because a player gets a lot of girls. I'm here to tell you that that's amateur. A player is not good with women, he's good at GETTING, he comes from a mentality of take.

A chooser on the other hand ATTRACTS. He works on himself regardless of the opinions of others and his actions and demeanor speak for him. That being said, we will discuss how having the right actions and demeanor is a matter of first changing who you are.

# Chapter 4 | Where to Start - The Power of Self-Improvement

*"More money does not solve money problems. Different relationships do not solve relationship problems. New work does not solve work problems... Money does not make you good with money. Love does not make you love yourself. Relationships don't make you good at relationships. Work does not make you good at your job or capable of work life balance. Problems don't inherently make you a stronger person unless you change and adapt. The variable is you. The common denominator is whether or not you shift your foundational perspective on the world and how you behave within it. Someone who makes $500k can be as seriously in debt and struggling as someone who makes $50k. And in fact, this happens more often than you think."*
**– Brianna Wiest**

Change happens at an identity level. Before we get into the life you should be building, let's get into the guy you don't want to be, because average is the enemy and good enough is the killer of great.

## The Average Joe

Joe wakes up in the morning and makes the first mistake of the day - snoozes his alarm. He gets out of bed, his room a mess, and leaves his bed a mess too. He goes to take a nice long shower and brush his teeth, still sleepy, and late to work. He speeds to work through traffic, getting annoyed at other drivers doing the same thing as him - driving. He gets to work, doesn't talk to many people, gets the job done, calls it a day, goes to happy hour after. At happy hour, he sees a girl he likes and stares at her. He decides to get the courage to go talk to her and goes up to offer her a free drink. She accepts and says "Nice to meet you" after getting her drink and leaves. Another one got away. He wanted her number because she was hot and he thought he could talk her up and take her out. It didn't work out. He goes back to his drink, gets another one and goes home to eat and watch TV on his couch. He falls asleep for a minute, then wakes up and goes to bed until tomorrow.

Does Joe seem fulfilled? Because he isn't, it's pretty clear. Would Joe be fulfilled if he was handed a million dollars and 20 hot girls to be in his life? No, because he would lose all of the money and all of the girls. Why? Because his character is not one of a person who has a million dollars and 20 female friends. He does average at his job, and puts no work into himself. On top of that, when he meets someone, he thinks about what he can take from them instead of what he can offer them. Did you pick up on that?

That's the most important part of getting you to the next level. You will become a man of value and someone who has something to offer, whether it's a smile, or a yacht.

Don't be Joe. Joe never invested in himself, and no one was there to tell him he should. The people around him are just like him, and he never felt the need to change, he's not happy, but he's comfortable. If that floats your boat, this book is not for you. Put it down, enjoy your life.

If you see something wrong with Joe's life, this book is for you, and the fact that you're still reading tells me that you're here to level up.

In life there are 3 progressions of identity everyone goes through. As we grow we are taught to associate our identity with what we HAVE, then as we mature we earn respect and attention based on what we DO, then finally we mature more and ultimately understand that our real value comes from who we are. The first two are finite and imply a limited self because they can both be measured. You can always not have enough, and not do enough, but you can't not BE enough because there is no measure on being, and this is the mindset you must understand and foster to achieve ultimate confidence.

Now, this doesn't mean you should yell affirmations in the mirror 10 times a day, it means start becoming. Start working on yourself to build the identity you look up to - the guy that girls want to have, and guys want to be. For the sake of this book, let's call this identity "The Chooser."

## The identity of the Chooser:

The Chooser is the guy that starts his day choosing himself first and foremost. He values his health, focuses on his career, makes time for people, and prioritizes his interests and the well-being of the people he loves. Looking good is one of his values. He makes an effort to stick to his disciplines and show up for himself daily. When it's time to work out, he works out. He doesn't tell himself that he'll do it next time because he already set the time for it and he's going to keep his promises. He gets places at the time he said he was going to get there if not earlier, and he follows through on his commitments once he has committed, even if other things come up. That's a major recipe: keeping your promises to yourself. Through this he learns to build up his sense of self and as a byproduct he develops high standards and confidence.

Because he keeps his promises regardless of his emotions, he trusts himself to do the same in daily situations that come up. This trust in yourself reinforces the belief "I will be ok, no matter what." At the end of the day, if you can't be there for yourself, you can't expect anyone else to. Because of this strong belief in himself, he walks around with a sense of calm and comfort in any social situation and it comes off so obviously in the way he walks, talks, shakes hands, breathes, and drinks. Even his gaze is comforting. His mind is in the right place, aligned with his intentions. Your physical health and discipline alone can skyrocket your average mood and confidence.

Having established his self-belief, the Chooser pursues his career with tenacity and determination knowing he can trust himself to be there for him when things get hard mentally. He is willing to take risks and to go for what he wants. He takes control of his life and is proactive about everything he commits to doing. He does not let life happen to him, but he plays a part in everything that happens. And when things go wrong he blames no one but himself. If something is against his principles and what he believes in, he is willing to walk away instead of sacrificing his values for his desires. Instead he either goes where he is wanted or creates his own environment.

The Chooser is the king of his domain. Everyone in his circle values and respects him as a leader. He chooses his friends and family over strangers and never goes out of his way to impress others. If he is out having a conversation with his friend and a girl interrupts them, he will not ignore his friend and forget about him in order to entertain her. He is not needy for attention because he is self-sufficient and has all the attention he needs from the people he cares about.

The Chooser fosters meaningful relationships even with people who are new in his life and does not objectify women as sex objects. He does not value sex over relationships and will turn it down if it questions his values. He is very selective with the people in his life because he has high standards that they need to live up to. He surrounds himself with strong and empowering people who build him up and foster a positive mindset.

The Chooser goes to bed content every night and wakes up inspired every morning. He pursues his goals and prioritizes his own needs before others'.

Notice how none of these qualities of the Chooser had anything to do with girls or what girls want. Ironically, that is what girls want - a leader who is grounded in himself and emotionally mature, not dependent on anyone's opinion of him.

Now the question is how do you reach this level? How do you build a social circle that respects you, develop the qualities of a leader, and the habits of a high level ambitious man?

The answer is a simple structure, but takes time to implement. The structure to follow is:

$$Be \rightarrow Do \rightarrow Have$$

Most people in this age associate their self worth with the validation from others which comes from either your accomplishments or the things you have that others want. So, naturally the structure they follow is:

$$Do \rightarrow Have \rightarrow Be.$$

Following that path you will go down an existential rabbit hole that brings you back to square one because the "Be" is not wholly dependent on doing or having. I'm saying this as someone who's dug himself into and out of the ditch several times and learned the hard way. I've made the mistakes that I talk about, that's why I am so confident in what I say.

DOING the right things will only get you so far until your true character comes out, and girls are built to sniff out that incongruence over time. If you only rely on tips and tricks to move you forward in an interaction, eventually she will be able to read it off of you because your micro-expressions will not be aligned with what you are saying. Girls are generally much better at reading micro-expressions than guys are, and that is something we have not yet learned to control consciously. So, unless you believe what you are saying based on your past experiences that have given you proof of what you are saying, don't say it. Instead focus on building the experiences in your personal life that will shape your identity.

BEING refers to cultivating a certain mindset, values, and qualities within yourself. This could include working on aspects such as self-confidence, self-awareness, emotional intelligence, and a positive mindset. Becoming the best version of yourself is a foundational step.

It's not about knowing the right techniques of what to say (doing), it's a matter of who you are and the beliefs you are operating from at a core level (being).

Once you start working on this you will find that the two of them intercept. That's because you can't sit by yourself at home and suddenly become someone else. The two are dependent on each other, but the belief comes first, and the doing is the reinforcement. The practical of doing this is to work on one thing at a time while getting real-world reference experience as supporting evidence for the new beliefs you are nurturing. The goal on this journey is to fully embrace and embody the new beliefs you are instilling. The more evidence you get, the stronger they will be ingrained.

What this looks like in a real world application is for example you want to instill the belief that "the world is a friendly place and people are nice to me." You would take every instance of someone being nice to you and interpret it in a way that is aligned with your new belief.

The best part about this is that you can talk to ninety-nine people who are mean to you and all you need is one successful interaction with someone being nice to you to use as a reference experience that the belief is possible, it exists, and it's true. That alone is enough to make a shift in your thinking and identity.

The HAVING comes later as you grow and mature with the BEING and DOING. When you "become" a Chooser, by establishing Chooser beliefs and "doing" the things that a Chooser does, then you will start "having" the things that a Chooser has, such as a big social circle full of people you love having around you.

But BEING is more than just instilling beliefs. It's about your relationship with yourself. As you develop this relationship, you will start discovering your most authentic self, finding things out about yourself that you don't like and learning to have compassion towards them. This process will shape your values, emotional intelligence, and mindset. You will learn to build self-acceptance and comfort with yourself the more aware you become. Then when you go out to make the effort to meet new people, they will sense your new energy before you have a chance to say a word. If you see yourself as a high value guy, they will sense and treat you like a high value guy, and you will reinforce the idea that you're a high value guy. It's a self-fulfilling cycle, and it starts from your self-talk and the stories you tell yourself about you based on your interpretation of events from your past and present.

# SECTION II

## APPLYING THE HIGH VALUE MINDSET

# CHAPTER 5 | The Framework

*"First we shape our tools, and thereafter our tools shape us."*
*- Marshall McLuhan*

With dating, as with all things, it's easier to establish discipline when it's already a part of your life. It's one thing to show up to the gym whenever you get a chance and it's another thing to be part of a team sport preparing for competition. Which do you think you will show up to more often? In the former scenario, you try to make your way into the gym every day, whereas in the latter scenario, you are accountable to other people. Sports are a big part of your life because you are competing and have a set daily schedule to follow.

Here's a more plain example. In what scenario will it be easier to lose weight? When your house is full of your favorite snacks? Or when you live right next to the organic food stores and healthy cafes in a neighborhood where people are health-conscious and seen exercising daily? In the former example, you will fall victim to your own thoughts and eventually lose willpower. In the latter example, even if you do have thoughts of cheating on your diet, you have more things keeping you accountable, one major one being that you don't have any snacks in the house to cheat with and all the stores nearby sell healthy things. On top of that, seeing others living a healthy life feeds the right thoughts in your mind. Seeing the results you want, being inspired by people, and also following the psychological principle of craving belonging and wanting to fit in will push you in the right direction almost effortlessly.

Progress is about your environment.

If you have approach-anxiety and have trouble carrying a conversation, it is much easier to talk to strangers and have something to say when you're out and about all day running errands, doing activities you enjoy, and keeping your mind active and observant. The opposite of this would be sitting at home or being in an office all day not talking to anyone or having any human contact and then going outside and being in your head when it comes to wanting to say something to a stranger.

Some will say "my job doesn't allow me to have human contact." That's a limiting belief. You must learn to play the cards you are dealt until you can get a new hand. Shift the way you do things, the places you frequent, and the people you're around to put yourself in more conversations daily. What if you don't know how to start conversations? That's the point. If you change your environment to go from no people to constantly surrounded by people, then conversations are more likely to spark up on their own until you can learn to create them yourself.

Now, in a case where you're literally working 24/7 with no human contact whatsoever, then you're screwed. You're in a bad environment at that point, time to change jobs. But, assuming you still have some influence over your daily life, here's the framework of how to develop your skills starting from below 0.

Environment is king. If you want to find wood you must go to where wood is abundant. But before you chop the wood, you must sharpen the ax. Environment is only the first step to a 3-step framework for developing yourself in this area. The next step is learning conversations in the full framework below:

1. Tailor Environment - Put yourself in environments where interactions are likely to happen

2. **Lead Conversations** - Learn to capitalize on those interactions that happen by chance

3. **Elevate Lifestyle** - Naturally create interactions, level yourself up, and maintain relationships

Once you master this framework, there will be no stopping you. You will become a "Chooser." The Chooser is the high value guy who is social and friendly and believes that the world is a friendly place as opposed to hostile. He is social and makes friends easily. He is a source of value, and everyone who comes in his path walks away better, whether their life changes or they leave with a tiny smile, his only intention is to give. He gives a type of respect to others that can only come from self-respect, and he expects the same treatment in return.

Let's break down an example of what this framework looks like as a day in the life of a Chooser named Bob.

Bob wakes up energized because he's ready to take on the challenges he has set for today and he was happy with his progress yesterday. Bob wakes up at the same time every day, rarely at the time of his alarm. He wakes up before his alarm because his body is accustomed to his routine lifestyle, so he's alert and doesn't need to snooze.

He gets up and goes to the gym no matter what the day brings, he's there to show up because that's who he is. He finishes his workout before getting started with his day. When he gets home he feels motivated from conquering his excuses in the morning and decides to add on to that by jumping into a cold shower to boost his mood, immune system, and testosterone levels. After 3 minutes in a cold shower, he takes a quick regular shower and goes to grab the clothes he set out last night. He's hyped and ready to go.

He gets dressed and goes to work. At work he's a joy to be around. He understands what people value and speaks to those values. He notices efforts where people wouldn't normally notice and he makes people feel appreciated and seen. The people he works with always want him around because his energy brings people up, the energy that he built up earlier in the day and every day before that.

When he gets off of work he stops by a coffee shop to work on other things he has going on. When he walks in he speaks to the cashier and addresses her by name. He notices she has an accent and comments on it. She says she's from Spain and they talk about travel for a bit. He puts in his order, adds a tip, and walks away leaving the cashier with a smile.

When he gets to his table he sees that his friends are texting him about plans for that night. They want to go out to a bar and catch up. Whenever they get together, they just vibe and laugh constantly.

They plan to get together and he gets back to work. At another table across there's a girl looking at him, he makes eye contact with her and gives her a gentle smile, she smiles back, and he slowly turns back to finish his work. After reaching a checkpoint in his work, he gets up to grab water and goes to introduce himself to the girl. She seems friendly and they find a lot in common so they decide to exchange contacts. They continue the conversation and he invites her to his table to have coffee together.

After their conversation he goes home to get ready for the night with his friends. The three of them are having a serious conversation when a girl interrupts his friend to make a comment and he tells her to hold on because his friend was discussing something with him. After their conversation, he sees a girl he likes standing with her friends and decides to approach them. He engages the whole group and makes sure everyone feels included in the conversation. He introduces his friends and asks the girl's friends if he and the girl can grab a drink for a minute. They go grab a drink and connect. He offers her his number and they continue the conversation. The girl's friends are leaving so she goes with them. He gets back to his friends.

That night he meets three other girls, not all of whom he's interested in romantically. On Sundays he typically likes to go hiking so he invited one of the girls along and they have plans for brunch after. Him and his friends go home and he has already made a new friend at the coffee shop and three more at the bar. He walks into any room with that level of confidence whether he's alone or with friends.

He didn't wake up this way out of nowhere. Throughout his life he learned to value the right things and prioritize himself and his growth over others. He does what he likes and he expresses himself authentically among strangers or friends. He values his health so he stays consistent at the gym. He values his enjoyment so he never goes on dates to places he wouldn't go alone. He values his growth so he is always looking for opportunities to develop further. He tends to his needs and never settles without knowingly choosing to and being happy with his decision. Every decision he makes is personal to him and everything in his life reflects who he is, from the water he drinks to the car he drives to the clothes he wears.

In this example, Bob picked the right environments to be in where he could meet the type of people he was interested in. He also knows how to start and lead a conversation based on his ability to meet women and follow up with incorporating them in his life. Lastly, he knows how to create opportunities and position himself correctly by sitting across from a table at the coffee shop with the girl he wanted to talk to and knowing how to engage her without saying anything before approaching and inviting her into his life because he has built a lifestyle for himself.

Bob was not an overnight success, it took time for him to develop. To become the Chooser you will need help in the process. Study those ahead of you so you can avoid their mistakes and expedite your growth.

# CHAPTER 6 | Environment - Get The F*ck Out of The House

*"It is not the critic who counts; not the man who points out how the strong man stumbles, or where the doer of deeds could have done them better. The credit belongs to the man who is actually in the arena, whose face is marred by dust and sweat and blood; who strives valiantly; who errs, who comes short again and again, because there is no effort without error and shortcoming."*
*– Theodore Roosevelt*

Showing up is the first step. If you want to change, you must either create or put yourself in environments where change is possible. You can't grow flowers in a drought. In the same way, you can't learn to lead conversations while never leaving your house to socialize.

Some people are understandably stuck in an office and don't have much flexibility in their daytime schedules to do much. However, they still have time to go home after work and watch TV. Others, work from home fully, or run their own business, but never leave the house. These are the same people that say they don't have time or the opportunity to work on themselves. However, either situation and all the situations in-between hold so much potential that people don't realize.

Your only excuse for not working on yourself would be if you are struggling to survive in the middle of nowhere, with no money or down time. Everyone else can work around their situation. And if you're stuck in an office with no people around, and live far from the city, then you can move and change jobs. It's not an easy solution, but it's also not a valid excuse.

I had a client living in Kansas. For the sake of privacy let's call this client Lance. Lance was an engineer living on the outskirts of the city, complaining to me that even if he put in the time and effort there was no one to approach and talk to. He worked from home much of the time, but he made it a priority to work on himself as well. He was a hard worker and was willing to do what it took to develop his skills.

We would learn all day how to talk and what to do, but he would rarely get interactions. Given, when he did have interactions they typically went well, but he wasn't able to get the results he wanted or establish a social circle.

It was time to make a big leap. I promised him that it was doable if he did what I told him and was willing to make the right changes. He did the right thing and put his trust in me.

We put together a game plan for him to organize and restructure his life in a way that would elevate him to where he wanted to be. It was going to be a big change but he was committed and I was with him on every step of the process. After some discussion and research, we ended up choosing Florida as the place that made the most sense and was most practical to move to. He had a few friends in Ft. Lauderdale that were of similar mind and similar goals as him, and we wanted to establish a tribe for him to grow with.

Over the next few weeks he started applying to remote jobs, looking for rentals, and reaching out to people. After some hard work, he found a rental and bought his flight to move. At the time, it was going to be a risk because he had not yet secured a job, but he decided to bet on himself and my guidance to get through it. He connected with a few friends and moved down to Florida. About two weeks had passed and he had not heard back from the company he had his heart set on. If he did not make something happen soon, it would be back to square one for us.

One thing about this skill is that learning how to talk to girls is the cherry on top. The real power of this skill comes in the form of learning how to communicate and move people in the direction you are trying to go. We constructed a plan for him to reach out and connect with hiring managers in the company he had applied to and establish a relationship. We ended up getting a phone call with one of the hiring managers, but he was not the person conducting interviews for the position.

Having prepped Lance on building rapport, leading conversation, and being memorable, he left an impression on the hiring manager. At the end of the phone call, he told Lance that he wasn't the one hiring for the position, but he will see what he can do because he deserves a shot. This is how we got Lance's foot in the door.

The hiring manager contacted the other hiring manager internally and sent him Lance's resume as a recommendation. The next day Lance heard back from the company and was invited to an interview. I'm sure you can guess how this story ends. Lance got the job and was able to stay in Ft. Lauderdale. The hard part was done.

Now that Lance was established in his new home, I told him to connect with his friends and share his goals with them. It turned out that one of the friends was networking with yacht owners in the area, and needed to put together a group to host a party. They split up the efforts to connect with the right people and get to work on meeting strangers and making new friends. The goal was to bring 8 girls to the yacht with the two guys plus the yacht owner.

Having practiced how to lead conversation, set up dates, and maintain relationships, he was able to invite the girls to the event they were hosting and the yacht owner was impressed. After the first event he offered his yacht to them whenever they needed it to host the same types of events. This shortly grew their network of yacht owners and female friends and this became a regular thing. Their other friends eventually wanted to take part, and now they are able to split resources and efforts to build out events and meet exponentially more people than they would have alone.

It's safe to say Lance's social life exploded once he moved to Florida, and with his newly developed skills, he is thriving with people.

In short, you must survey your life and take into account everything you have going on, all your responsibilities, and commitments. Then, figure out what you can shift around and what you can change completely to be more aligned with your goals. In this instance, it's getting you out in public more often and choosing the right places to go. This includes even grocery shopping. Everything must be aligned with the lifestyle and habits of the future you.

In all endeavors you must first envision the goal you're trying to reach and then break down the steps to get there. In this case, that means taking a look at the vision you see for yourself, and who you want to be in the future, including who you want to be surrounded by. Envision those people, the things they do, the places they frequent, the things you do together, and what your interactions look like. Your goal is to find those people in the present. Once you find them, figure out their values and see if all of that is aligned with the vision you created for yourself.

Sometimes, what happens is that people realize that the vision they had of the future life that they would be living isn't actually the life that they want, and the people that they are surrounded by aren't people that they are on the same page with in terms of beliefs, values, and lifestyle. Some people see others having fun, especially on social media, and think that the reality of having that life will be something they want without realizing the behind-the-scenes of not only the work that goes into that but also the results that come with it. The fun is only a glimpse of someone's lifestyle.

For example, a lot of people look up to celebrities, but what they don't see is the mental health issue that's going on in the backend, they don't see the drugs that most celebrities are exposed to, especially don't see the work that goes into reaching that level and the things that those celebrities have to go through and deal with. Fame isn't always a good thing, but it always looks good from the outside and then reality you could envision that life for yourself, but deep down, you just want a deep connection with another human being and intimacy. So when people start to work their way up to the lifestyle that they envision for themselves, sometimes they take a turn and step back to focus on themselves and cleanse their circle of the people that are a bad influence on them.

What I'm trying to say is that on this journey you will make a lot of decisions and change a lot more of them, but keeping your environment the same will never move you forward, because realizing what you want is part of the journey.

Once you have a system for putting yourself in environments, you must then adapt. This means learning how to carry and lead conversations when interactions strike up.

# CHAPTER 7 | Leading Part 1 - Starting & Approach Anxiety

*"Ego is the enemy - giving us wicked feedback, disconnected from reality. It's defensive, precisely when we cannot afford to be defensive. It blocks us from improving by telling us that we don't need to improve."*
**- Ryan Holiday**

When guys do a bootcamp with me for the first time, a lot of them hit an ego block because typically no one has pushed their boundaries before. Naturally, this brings up a lot of resistance and we spend time tackling that resistance and breaking it down, mentally and physically. Even the most humble guys eventually realize that their ego, their sense of who they are, fights them when they've reached the point where change happens.

When you hit the point of failure in a workout and your mind tells you to stop, that's where the growth happens. People who work out by simply going through the motions and leaving once they get tired are the ones that waste their time or take forever to develop their bodies. In reality, it's all a mental game. Your mind resists doing one more set when you're tired the same way it resists approaching a stranger when you've lived your whole life only talking to people you know, never pushing your boundaries.

To break down your ego, you must challenge your sense of identity and eventually kill it to become someone new. That's the very definition of change, and the ego hates change because it has evolved to seek familiarity and comfort.

I had a client that was such a charismatic conversationalist and actually fun to talk to. I had him roleplay with a girl and her feedback to him was that she was invested in the conversation with him. The problem came when he had to approach a stranger. I challenged him to run up to someone and open a conversation and because he was nervous about being able to talk to a girl, he would resort to his functional conversation topics like asking for directions and leaving shortly after. I explained to him that his mind is fighting him because it considers those functional conversation topics safe so it's hard for him to take a "risk" to actually approach and be direct.

I pointed out that it's actually weird for him to run up to someone to ask for directions because there is no justification behind it since he could have asked anyone around him, and he's putting himself at a disadvantage by doing that because that's just another unspoken objection that he has to address. It wasn't until I told him that his mind was choosing a familiar hell over an unfamiliar heaven that he realized he was self-sabotaging.

After gaining that awareness, not only did he become more open to the act of striking up conversation with a stranger, but the girls were much more receptive to his approach and it drove the point home for him. Sometimes, all it takes is becoming aware of the resistance to overcome it.

## Dave's story

When students start giving me excuses and resistance to approaching someone, picking and choosing instead of taking action, I will do something to snap them out of their patterns and break their limiting beliefs. In the case of Dave, he was under the impression that it's weird to go up to someone and when he did talk to them he would think that they are either being sarcastic in their response or mocking and laughing at him.

This was a serious case because I had to challenge his whole reality at that point. As a Chooser, you have to be comfortable having conviction and commanding attention because strong men don't shy away from failure or embarrassment which is a very masculine and attractive quality.

Dave loved to be passive, even in his friend circles. He didn't feel comfortable putting himself out there, being loud and assertive. So, that's exactly what he had to do. Your mindset doesn't just change by meditating on new beliefs, to be a Chooser you have to act like one too. The moment you step into that new identity, your mind will start fighting you, but at the same time it will be shifting your thoughts to adapt to the new environment or "way of being" that you put it in.

You can speed up this process by consciously shifting your thoughts and looking for external evidence to reinforce it. So, I had to build the external situation for him and guide him on how to interpret it from the perspective of a Chooser. I had him approach in the most uncomfortable way possible - running up to someone walking in the middle of a crowd and getting her attention way ahead of starting the actual conversation.

Dave's limiting beliefs made him think that if he called out to a girl from further away to get her attention, she would not notice him and if she didn't respond then he would give up feeling rejected when in reality he was so soft spoken that the girls wouldn't even hear him. Some girls would turn around a few seconds after he had tried to get their attention because they thought someone was talking to them, but Dave had already given up and started walking away. He was so afraid of that rejection that he rejected himself first before the girl had a chance to reject him so that he could avoid the pain of being turned away. Not only did he not want to command attention from the girl, but he was also afraid that the people around would hear him and he would have more pressure to not look bad in front of everyone. His ego was trying hard to protect him, as is its evolutionary role.

After some time conditioning new beliefs, he started to understand and embrace new perspectives. Dave had no idea he could be confident enough to command attention or persist when he didn't get a response. Everyone thinks it's needy to look like you're trying to get a girl's attention, but it's needy only when it's coming from a needy place. A confident man goes for what he wants and he is not afraid to make it known without getting his ego tied up in the results, but in simply giving himself permission to make his own needs a priority.

Imagine someone had your wallet and you were trying to run up to them and get their attention before they walked away. You wouldn't be thinking about looking needy because your wallet is important and your intention to get it back would be a priority. In the same way, your emotions are important and deserve to be a priority. Having the drive and ambition to go for what you want while knowing how to be calibrated and respectful is an attractive quality. It shows your social awareness, yet value in yourself.

Dave had no idea he could be confident enough to get a girl's attention from further away, much less persist if she didn't hear him. All it took was challenging the beliefs that he had never been willing to question because he was conditioned to accept them.

## Never Run Out of Things to Say

After being able to get a girl's attention and face their fear of approaching and starting conversation, most guys run out of things to say, and the ones who don't just stack question after question until the girl gets bored and walks away. So then the question becomes, what do you say to have an engaging conversation and see the girl again? This is usually where people blank out.

Know that the start is always going to be rocky. You can't plan the whole thing out because even if you do, you don't know how the person will respond until you start the conversation. I've seen girls looking angry that light up after an approach and I've seen girls looking happy or neutral that shut down a conversation before it starts. The point is: figure it out after starting.

So, don't overthink it, a simple "Excuse me, I wanted to say hi. I'm John," does the trick. Oftentimes, that's a good starting point in itself. Remember, the start will be rocky no matter what, but the good news is that your opener isn't what your future wife is going to remember on your wedding day, what she will remember is how you made her feel when she met you.

I hope you understand by now that the most important thing is just taking action. But I understand. Some people can't get themselves to open their mouth and speak a word to begin with. Some people deal with massive approach anxiety and it can feel almost paralyzing to even take the first step. That's because, like my client Dave, we're so tied up in our sense of identity and what people will think of us. So you won't be surprised when I tell you the first step starts way before you even see the girl.

The would have, could have, should have, what does that mean? You don't wanna live in the would have, could have, should have world. A world where you will never know what could have happened, so your imagination runs wild on the endless possibilities that could have been, and you start to feel regret because you never did it. You never found out what could have been. Don't be that guy, please. Take action. Do it. Don't live in the would have, could have world, it's a crappy world to live in.

One of my clients - let's call him Vincent, was a doctor with many scholarly achievements under his belt. He was on the Dean's list in college, got his PhD from a top university, and got an MBA in the middle of med school. He even took improv classes and started performing with a team of people on stage. Vincent was the type of person that was good at everything he did. He had different coaches and therapists and had even invested in private live coaching, but still struggled with the idea of talking to women and staying in touch. There was something deeper holding him back from opening himself up fully. After he had spent thousands of dollars into his personal development, he met me and I pulled up my sleeves because I knew this was going to be a challenge, but I knew how to help him.

We spent the next few months drilling and practicing conversation skills so that he knew exactly what to say when the opportunity arose. He was very witty and charismatic in conversation when he felt comfortable. On the lucky occasions he would get into a conversation and felt accepted and safe, he would turn into the most charming guy and the girl would love him every time. But for him to start a conversation he would have to be naturally pushed into it either by the girl inviting or initiating conversation or me starting one and bringing him into it.

We had practiced every conversation exercise there was, but he couldn't approach on his own. He was stuck on the first phase of the framework - putting himself in the environments where conversation can happen. I had to do something to break his walls down and get him to open up.

What Vincent was lacking wasn't the skill or the status, he had both. What he was lacking was momentum, because his ego was trying to protect him and when the moment presented itself, the resistance from his ego was too strong to break in an instance and jump in.

One day I told him to reach out to me the moment he wakes up and we're going to spend the day together. "Jumping in" was going to be the theme of our time together that day. I knew the things holding him back, I just had to find a way to get to that deeper part of him. I gave him little tasks to do and we spent the entire morning overcoming his resistance by himself. In the afternoon he went to meet with a friend of his who I had gotten to know as well. While they were out, I received a text from his friend "What are you teaching this guy?" I knew at that point that I had broken through. Then he said "He just went up to two beautiful women and struck up a conversation without me having to say a word."

It was one of my proudest moments because I knew how long he was stuck with this issue and how much he struggled to overcome it and the frustrations that came with constantly hitting the wall with other coaches.I saw the bigger picture where Vincent was about to go. His resistance was officially broken, we found a crack, and now we could work with it. The rest of our time together was going to be upward progress.

A month after that event, he was out on his own approaching and talking to women and all I had to do that time was challenge him to do it. I didn't need to push him or spend the day on the phone with him, he just did it.

The thing with Vincent was that he had a lot of success in his field, and that was the very reason he had trouble approaching and conversing with women. His identity was built upon his successes, and he was afraid to challenge it. I had to dig deep to address the thing holding him back without him realizing it until he started getting results and picking up enough momentum to overcome his barriers himself and it worked like a charm. The key is just starting, but if you need to build up to that, resort to micro-momentum.

Once you get used to taking action and starting, the barrier of entry needs to be as low as possible for you to get into a conversation easily. Once you're in, your brain will have to figure it out, and it does (much like how taking action for discipline works). Whether you say the smoothest line, or a simple "Hi," it's going to start off rocky anyway. Most guys think about the best thing to say and how to go about it, trying to calibrate to the situation and read the person before even knowing who the person is. You will never know who she is or how she will react until she does. You cannot calibrate to her until you have entered her bubble and opened a conversation. Until you are in a conversation, all you're seeing is the default look on people's faces that says nothing about who they are internally or what approach they would respond well to. You have to just trust in your abilities to adapt, but most of all, trust in the fact that you have value to offer.

A good rule of thumb is start the conversation, then calibrate. Think "ready, fire, then aim." You're going to be firing again, each time your aim will improve. In a conversation context it's "ready, open, then calibrate." As you open more interactions with people and sharpen your aim by calibrating, you're going to have better and more calibrated ways of starting. No matter how calibrated you become though, it will always be a little rocky at first. Beginnings are always rocky, that seems to be a rule of life.

Once you build a habit of starting before knowing what to do and where to take the conversation, then you can worry about how to best handle different situations and where to lead it.

Since this chapter is about leading, we're going to go over some fundamental ways of keeping the conversation going without putting any pressure on yourself, even when you get stuck, but the first step is the most important - open, then calibrate.

I met one of my close female friends while walking my dog one morning, let's call her Sarah. Yes, we dated too, but decided to keep it in the friendzone. More about that later.

She was walking to her car when my puppy and I were passing by. She looked at my dog and I opened a conversation with a comment. She came closer to see my dog and we started talking, but the conversation stopped and she got quiet for a second. Seconds felt like minutes as I panicked about what to say next and how to keep the conversation from dying out.

My mind was blanking out and it was as if I forgot how to speak because of the anxiety building up. I thought it was over, because it felt like she was about to walk away, but she stayed an extra second before leaving and in that moment I thought to myself "Just say one more thing." All I did was make one more comment. The conversation continued smoothly as if it hadn't been interrupted at all and the rest is history. I knew for a fact we were in conversation rather than that transitional period where you're making small talk and either of you can walk away at any moment.

The reason that was a learning moment for me, was because most guys tend to leave the interaction thinking the girl doesn't want to talk and they have nothing relevant to say, but leaving the interaction only reinforces that belief. That moment I proved that belief wrong and established a new belief, and that is the process I teach now. Test the waters, say one more thing, because you never know if the girl is just as nervous as you wanting to continue the conversation but doesn't know what to say, which is the case more than you know.

No, there was no magical line to re-engage the conversation, it was a simple observation, but most guys will still overthink this process. Observations are all around you whether it's based on the physical world around you or the internal world of your emotions, it's simply a matter of being aware of them. When we get nervous we tend to zone out and blank out in fear of saying the wrong thing. Next time you encounter a situation like getting stuck in your head, switch your brain on for an instance and challenge yourself to make a single statement.

In my case, during the instance of the interaction, it was 6 a.m., I hadn't slept so I was feeling tired, my dog wasn't acting aggressive and seemed to be taking a liking to her, she was wearing gym clothes and seemed like she worked out because she was in shape and up so early, she was carrying a hoodie in her hand, she had her car keys in the other hand. There was so much happening there, and enough context to keep a conversation going.

Given all that information, what comment can you make that would re-engage conversation?

You might have noticed I emphasize statements and comments as opposed to asking questions. Most people tell you to ask questions to get the girl talking about herself, but if a girl does not know you, you're doing too much with the questioning. You don't want to turn it into an interview. Instead you want to offer a statement in the form of an observation, opinion, or story and invite her to contribute to the conversation by adding to what you have to say with a story or opinion of her own to fuel the conversation. Know that the world is a friendly place, and people are willing to stay and have conversation with you if you offer them conversation.

If you take nothing else from this chapter, read and reread that paragraph until you have a full grasp on the concept of giving value in a conversation in the form of statements not questions. That is absolutely important.

Now that we've established that statements rule over questions any day of the week, let's break down what statements can look like and how you can keep an engaging conversation going without running out of things to say.

## The ROOTS Method

If you've researched online about keeping a conversation going, you might have come across the FORD method (Family, Occupation, Recreation, Dreams) or something similar. As is the case with many gurus online, this advice is out of context. What they will say is that you should ask these types of personal questions with the goal of getting the girl to talk about herself because "girls love to talk about themselves" and these are open-ended questions, etc. Though there is some validity to this advice, it's so out of context that guys will find articles and videos on the subject and go try these techniques on girls and get frustrated when girls don't give them the time of day or give them super short answers to be nice before leaving.

First of all, this method can easily lead the conversation into feeling like an interview, and second of all it's not geared toward small talk and banter, it more naturally fits into the connection phase of the interaction once you've built a solid amount of rapport with the person. Therefore, I wouldn't rely on this method as your source of conversation until later on in the interaction when you've shown her who you are and are then getting to know her. Even then I wouldn't fully rely on it as conversations around occupation can suck you in and get very logical very quickly, sometimes without even noticing. At the end of it you'll be left thinking that you had a great long conversation but she never got back to you after that.

So how do you have a conversation from start to finish? What are the key concepts involved? You already know that your focus should be sticking to statement based conversation, especially in the beginning, but what does that look like?

We've emphasized one aspect, which was making observations based on the physical environment and your internal state. Another aspect of conversation includes debating over engaging opinions, especially on the topic of relationships and psychology. You can even ask for an opinion on something that you're genuinely debating in your mind and want to get another person's perspective on. This is the beauty of being the "Chooser" because the Chooser has a lot going on in his day and a lot of interesting situations to grasp onto in conversation with others. The key is to stay open minded throughout your days on things that come up that spark your curiosity and you'd like another person's feedback on. This way the conversation is also more spontaneous and natural to you.

Another factor of the Chooser having an interesting life in the day-to-day, is that he has stories to tell about things that were out of the ordinary. Maybe he went to a networking event earlier that day and the lounge had a beautiful view. Maybe he found a little gem coffee shop that not a lot of people know about that he can share in conversation. There is so much that goes on that all you really need to do is be aware of it and learn to engage people in the way you talk about past events with your tonality and body language. More on this later. The material is otherwise all there, you already have it.

Stories help you relate to the person as you exchange interesting information about yourselves and connect on things that you find in common. Telling stories also overlaps with opinions and observations as you can use both strategically to bring the girl into your story and keep it more engaging. You can cut yourself off to make an observation and bring the conversation to her, or you can get an opinion on what you're talking about to bring her into the conversation. You can also give your own opinions in the sname way or either empower or validate hers if you agree with them. Empowering a person is a powerful way of encouraging more of what they are doing, which usually leads them to talk more about the subject you've shown enthusiasm towards.

The next aspect of conversation is a little more advanced and takes more skills to deliver with proper timing and accuracy. The concept is teasing. If you know how to challenge a girl in the right way, it can make a world of a difference in your attraction. Knowing how to emotionally stimulate people in general is a superpower that is a big aspect of influence whether it's in your job or in your social life. I won't get too deep into the calibration that goes into teasing and the ability of creating a push-and-pull with proper timing because that comes over time with practice.

These are the key factors of the beginning of a conversation and a much better way of keeping the conversation engaging than asking questions with the FORD method.

The ROOTS method stands for Relating, Observations, Opinions, Teasing, and Stories. We didn't touch on Relating but that's pretty self-explanatory. When the other person shares something, see if you can reciprocate by relating to what they said and this will help you build rapport. We touched on everything else, but there's one thing that requires diving deeper into because it's such a common issue - teasing. We'll break this down in the next chapter.

# CHAPTER 8 | Leading Part 2 - Chemistry & Tension

*"If no resistances or obstacles face you, you must create them. No seduction can proceed without them."*
**- Robert Greene, The Art of Seduction**

Like Robert Greene said, there needs to be a challenge, some type of obstacle, a push and pull in an interaction that makes it fun to "play." That's where attraction is built. It's what we call having "chemistry" with someone.

Let's talk about chemistry. What is chemistry? How do you build chemistry? Can you fake it? Where does it come from?

A common issue people come to me for is platonic conversation. Students who are newly learning how to build attraction say "Gor, I can go up to girls, I can talk to girls, I can carry conversations, but no matter what I do my conversations go nowhere and the ones that do go somewhere usually end up in the friendzone." First of all, I don't believe in the friendzone and you shouldn't either. The dynamic between a man and a woman is just that - dynamic. It ebbs and flows and you can control the level of tension between you. If you remember the character of the Chooser, not once was there any mention of ending up in the friendzone or avoiding the friendzone, there was only a mention of value. The Chooser adds value to everyone with no expectation to get something, especially in a way that disrespects or objectifies women. We are all human, and all experience dynamic emotions, and varying roles in each other's lives. Men must stop seeing women as someone they would have sex with or not have sex with. Women have much more to add into a man's life than that, but as two opposite sexes there will always be some level of sexual tension underneath whether anyone acts on it or not. Knowing how to build more of that sexual tension deliberately is basically the path of building attraction.

So when you're stepping into the world of dating, one of the most subtle, yet most powerful skills you can develop is the art of teasing and flirting. At first glance, these might seem like playful, innocuous parts of conversation. But dive a little deeper, and you'll find they're the very threads that can weave attraction, connection, and intrigue in the tapestry of your interactions.

In this chapter, we're going to explore the nuances of teasing and flirting. You'll learn not just what they are, but how to use them effectively to create a connection that goes beyond just a casual chat. It's about striking the right balance, using emotional intelligence, and understanding the subtle art of 'push and pull' in conversation. Teasing is a dance of banter, a subtle interplay of words that involves both pushing boundaries and pulling back, creating a dynamic and engaging exchange.

Teasing and flirting are like the dance of conversation. They add a playful, engaging dynamic to your interactions, making them more memorable and impactful. But as with any skill, there's a fine line between doing it just right and missing the mark.

Teasing and flirting share a common thread in that both involve playful interaction and often a degree of wit or humor. However, flirting takes things a step further by introducing a romantic or sexual undertone to the conversation. Let's explore how teasing and flirting are related and how flirting adds that extra layer of attraction.

Teasing can be thought of as the foundation of flirting. It sets the stage for a dynamic and engaging interaction. When you tease someone, you're creating a sense of playfulness and rapport. It's a way to show that you're comfortable with each other and can exchange light-hearted banter. Teasing is like adding a dash of spice to your conversation. It starts to introduce tension, ignites interest, and keeps things engaging. Imagine you're chatting with someone you find attractive. You've overcome the initial hesitation, and now it's time to inject some fun into the interaction.

I want to introduce you to Sam. He's one of my clients that I'm currently coaching and we were talking about chemistry.

So Sam, he's really good, and I mean really good at keeping the conversation going. Girls constantly tell him he's fun to talk to and they would react well to him. So the girls would be receptive to him, and Sam has no fear of approaching any girl, so he is constantly meeting new women and he gets a good reaction, he keeps the conversation going, doesn't really run out of things to say, but the big problem is that he lacked chemistry with women, there was no sexual tension, there was no man to woman energy. So while he was good at staying in the conversation, at times it would feel redundant, like someone driving a car on the freeway and not having a destination, just driving to drive, that's what it felt like. So here's what was missing, let's dive into the solution.

Sam was so nice and friendly that he was uncomfortable with the idea of pushing a girl away. Not only that, but he would leave an interaction at the first sign of it dying down. Here's what got him to the next level. When you push a girl in an interaction it offers her a challenge that excites her because it feels like she is earning your attention.

I was so determined to get him to overcome his challenges that I got on the phone with him and stayed with him the entire time he was out. What ended up happening was a surprisingly quick turn of events.

After a few interactions to warm up being open and social, we ended up in a conversation with one girl that was receptive to him just like all the other girls, but there was something different about this one. When Sam would make a joke or act cocky she would laugh and empower him. I told him right then that she was showing a lot of interest and that he is not allowed to leave that conversation or I was going to be mad. I could hear the girl's responses and guided him through the parts where he would usually fall off. We ended up giving the girl his instagram and setting up a date that same night.

That evening, we got on another call and went over how to run his date and here are all the things that he did right and that you can do too when you start applying this.

We planned the logistics with two goals in mind: move to multiple locations throughout the date and make sure that each location is closer in the direction of his house in case she ended up going back with him.

I had him choose the first venue with the goal of two things: setting an intimate mood and showing man to woman intention. To set an intimate mood we looked up a venue with a layout where they could move around, a possible activity they could do like taking photos in a photobooth, and dim lighting to make it romantic. As they interacted with the environment, he was to increase the intimacy gradually by introducing touch and pulling away based on the girl's comfort and receptivity without getting to a point where she pushed him away.

This paired with his willingness to sexualize conversation allowed him to build tension with the girl and that tension is where all the attraction is built. They ended up kissing at the first venue and getting ice cream afterwards, which breaks and resets the tension to be built up again. The cycling of this tension building makes the attraction stronger each time. They ended up going back to his place and spent the night together.

Central to effective teasing is the concept of 'push and pull.' This is where things get interesting.

## The Push

The "push" in teasing is the element that introduces an unexpected twist into the conversation. It involves throwing in a witty remark or a playful comment that catches the other person off guard. The push is the spice that adds excitement, making the interaction more interesting and memorable. It's not about being hurtful; rather, it's about injecting a bit of surprise into the conversation.

You gently 'push' the other person away with a playful joke or a light-hearted jab. This isn't about being mean or offensive; it's a playful push.

## The Pull

On the flip side, the "pull" is the reassuring element that follows the push. It's about ensuring that the other person feels comfortable and in on the joke. The pull creates a warm atmosphere, counteracting any coolness introduced by the push. It's the aftermath that brings a sense of camaraderie, emphasizing that the teasing is all in good fun. The push and pull work in tandem, creating a dynamic rhythm within the conversation.

You 'pull' them back with a smile, a compliment, or some indication that you're just kidding.

The idea here is to create a dynamic that is playful and engaging. For instance, you might say, "You're such a nerd for loving Star Wars so much... but I've got to admit, that's also kind of cool." Here, the 'push' is calling them a nerd, and the 'pull' is acknowledging that their interest is cool.

The key to successful teasing lies in balance and understanding the other person's boundaries. Teasing should always be done in good spirit. If they're smiling, laughing, or playfully hitting back with their own tease, you're on the right track. Stay clear of topics that could be hurtful or too personal.

Good teasing involves both parties. If you're the only one doing the teasing, it's not a playful interaction; it's just you talking at someone.

Teasing, when done right, builds a connection and shows that you're comfortable enough with someone to engage in light-hearted banter. It's not about proving a point or being superior; it's about adding a bit of playful zest to the conversation.

Now that you know what builds attraction and what you're supposed to do to get there, here are some applicable ways you can use it for yourself.

- "You are the coolest person I have met... in the last 5 minutes."

- "You are so nice... It's never going to work between us."

- "I don't like you... What I mean by that is I fucking love you."

Take into consideration that delivery is super important with these, and that these are basic level lines for an advanced level skill, but let these serve as an introductory example of the push and pull you're going for in order to build attraction. You can do this in different ways as long as there is a variation of emotions. The worst thing you can have is indifference, because that resembles a stagnant emotion.

Any form of positive or negative emotion will build investment from the woman, but overdoing either will lose the interaction.

## Keeping it Light

A crucial aspect of mastering the teasing dance is keeping it light. The primary goal is to evoke laughter, not drama. Teasing should feel like a feather, not a sledgehammer—playful, not hurtful. It's about creating an atmosphere where everyone involved feels at ease, contributing to the overall enjoyment of the interaction. The key is to strike a balance that adds fun without crossing into uncomfortable territory.

Teasing is akin to a playful exchange, a cat and mouse game where one person throws a tease, and the other reacts. It creates a continuous and engaging chase within the conversation, fostering a lively and dynamic atmosphere. This cat and mouse dynamic keeps the interaction interesting, ensuring that both parties actively participate in the banter. It's a form of verbal sparring that contributes to the overall enjoyment of the teasing dance.

This might sound repetitive, but I need you to understand that the woman should never ever feel insulted by your comments or remarks. If she gets insulted, then you are doing it wrong. Remember, pushing and pulling are advanced tactics, so you have to make sure that your tonality and body language are on point when you deliver them.

Now, let's delve into a brief example to illustrate the dynamics of teasing in action.

## The Teasing Tango: A Story Example

Picture a rooftop bar with a vibrant atmosphere. You're sharing drinks with your friend, Sarah, and the teasing begins.

You take a casual sip of your drink, a playful grin on your face. "Any good jokes lately?"

Sarah raises an eyebrow, a smirk forming on her lips. "Dad humor again?"

You chuckle, "Maybe, but your laugh is the real joke."

She playfully rolls her eyes, "You think you're a comedian after one open mic night."

Leaning back with confidence, you quip, "Had the crowd in stitches. You're just jealous."

Her smirk widens, "Jealous? I've seen funnier memes."

The banter continues in this teasing tango, with each push met by a pull. Laughter fills the air as the exchange unfolds, creating an engaging and enjoyable interaction between friends.

Teasing, with its push and pull dynamics, is a dance within conversations. It's about injecting surprise while ensuring everyone involved feels comfortable and engaged. Keeping it light and playful, the art of teasing contributes to the overall enjoyment of social interactions. So, find that sweet spot, embrace the teasing dance, and let the banter unfold with laughter and camaraderie.

Flirting is the same thing as teasing, except with a sexual undertone. Flirting is where you show sexual interest in the other person. It can be the same fun and playful lines, but with a twist of adding intention to the mix. It's about subtly hinting at your desires and creating a charged atmosphere that ignites passion. However, it's essential to approach this aspect of flirting with sensitivity and respect, ensuring that both parties are comfortable and consenting to the dynamic.

When incorporating a sexual undertone into your flirting, it's crucial to gauge the other person's response and adjust your approach accordingly. Pay attention to their body language and verbal cues to ensure that they're receptive to the flirtatious banter.

One way to introduce a sexual undertone is through suggestive language and playful innuendos. These can be subtle hints or more explicit references, depending on the comfort level and rapport you've established with the other person. Remember to keep it light and playful, avoiding anything that may come across as crude or disrespectful.

Another approach is through physical touch. A gentle brush of the hand, a lingering gaze, or a playful tap on the shoulder can convey your attraction and desire in a subtle yet unmistakable way. Again, it's essential to respect boundaries and ensure that the other person is comfortable with physical contact.

Ultimately, flirting with a sexual undertone is about creating a sense of anticipation and excitement, building towards a deeper connection and potentially, a more intimate encounter. However, it's crucial to proceed with caution and always prioritize mutual consent and respect in your interactions. When done right, flirting with a sexual undertone can add a thrilling edge to your interactions and pave the way for a more passionate connection.

# CHAPTER 9 | Leading Part 3 - Building Connection

*"I've learned that people will forget what you said, people will forget what you did, but people will never forget how you made them feel."*
**– Maya Angelou**

Once you gain social freedom, you will be amazed at what people you meet. I have met so many new people that have led to the most wonderful experiences. I've gotten to travel and have a place to stay and experience the destination from a local perspective. I've been invited to events for free. I've been a guest with celebrities at fashion shows and other events. Beyond the amazing experiences, I have met some amazing people that have given me new perspectives on life and helped me grow as a person. Those who see the bigger picture know that having these social skills is never about getting laid, it's a matter of connecting with people, and even deeper it's a matter of opening yourself up to receive that love and connection. At the end of the day this journey always revolves around who you become in the process.

After facing a hundred rejections, all it takes is that one person for you to think to yourself "Wow, I could have lived my entire life having no idea this person existed, never having experienced this... who knew this existed, who knew this adventure was possible, who knew they would impact my life this way, and bring out that part of me I thought was hidden away." That's how some of the greatest businesses are started, and relationships are made.

I explained this concept to one of my clients at one of our retreats. Let's call him Leo. Leo had a lot of life experience on top of his education. He had a PhD from a top tier school and had worked at multiple top tier tech companies. He also had different professions and hobbies throughout his life, so besides his specializations, he knew a little about a lot of things. He was very personable and interesting to talk to because he offered so much new insight and perspective.

Leo was hitting a huge mental block every time it came to approaching women. He was very sophisticated and knowledgeable, had a lot of life experience, and could keep a conversation going for hours when he felt comfortable, but he could not approach, hook, and flirt. He would only talk to the girls when I would merge him into a conversation, and even then he would exit quickly, thinking that the girl doesn't want to talk to him or that there's nothing relevant to talk about.

I wanted to prove a point to Leo, something that would leave an engrained memory in him to always refer back to. I told him to come with me and walked him into a coffee shop. Just in that moment, there was a girl there getting water and it was the perfect teaching opportunity. By the time I turned around to tell him to approach her, he was in a conversation with someone he knew and would not leave even though it was getting dragged on. It was a familiar situation for him, he went back into his comfort zone, and the girl left.

We went back across the street and I was disappointed. As I was telling him about how every person carries their own story and you never know who you will meet and how they will impact your life, I noticed the same girl sitting on a bench where we came from across the street. I told him you have a second chance and he was still stuck in his head.

While going through all that resistance in his head, and overthinking the situation as to what the girl will say, or how he should approach her, he saw me turn around and walk to her. It turned out that she was a fashion model that had won multiple Miss Universe competitions and was waiting for her Uber after grabbing coffee in a plain coffee shop. We exchanged contact info and continued the conversation. He saw me from across the street having a fun conversation with the girl who was seemingly "unapproachable" sitting on her own with a straight face.

I wasn't saying any magic words or doing any special tricks to make her laugh, I was only bringing who I was to the table and being comfortable with the uncomfortable, focused on giving not taking. After seeing that, Leo approached anyone I would tell him to without question or argument.

By the end of our time together that day, we had gone to eat and he was in over an hour long conversation with a girl he walked up to by the beach and eventually came back with the biggest smile on his face.

I left him with a word that is at the core of why I am passionate about what I do. The word is "sonder." So if you need a reason to be social, here's something you can put on your wall.

"Sonder - The realization that each random passerby is living a life as vivid and complex as your own — populated with their own ambitions, friends, routines, worries and inherited craziness — an epic story that continues invisibly around you like an anthill sprawling deep underground, with elaborate passageways to thousands of other lives that you'll never know existed, in which you might appear only once, as an extra sipping coffee in the background, as a blur of traffic passing on the highway, as a lighted window at dusk."

## How To See Her Again

So, you've kicked off a conversation and you're starting to click. Nice work! Now, let's talk about  ensuring the initial connection leads to further meetings using what I like to call the CHIL method, which stands for Common Ground, Hobbies, Interests, and Logistics.

### Common Ground

Identifying mutual interests is crucial because it provides a logical basis for suggesting another meeting. For instance, discovering a shared appreciation for a specific genre of music or a type of cuisine can naturally lead to planning a date related to these interests. The aim is to use these shared points as a foundation for suggesting a second meeting, making it seem like a natural extension of your conversation.

### Hobbies

Understanding her hobbies offers insight into her preferences and personality, serving as potential activities for when you meet. If she mentions enjoying outdoor activities and you know a great hiking spot, proposing a hike as your next meet-up can offer a personalized touch to your suggestion, indicating thoughtfulness and attentiveness to her interests.

### Interests

Diving deeper into specific interests allows for more cultivated activity suggestions. Not only that, it also gives you an idea of her values and the types of conversation topics she's into. Maybe she really loves traveling and you just got back from a trip. You can open up a new thread of conversation, you can show her pictures, you can make plans, either on the spot or when you meet again. Either way you get a good idea of what she's all about and where you can take this relationship.

### Logistics

Addressing logistics is about acknowledging practical considerations for a follow-up. It involves being mindful of her schedule and proposing a meeting time and place that accommodates both parties. Demonstrating flexibility and consideration in planning shows respect for her time and a genuine interest in facilitating the meeting.

In applying the CHIL method, the goal is to strategically leverage the initial connection to plan a follow-up. It involves a blend of personal insight and practical planning, ensuring that the suggestion for another meeting is both appealing and feasible. This approach not only helps you lead to possible future interactions but also positions you as thoughtful and considerate, increasing the likelihood of a positive response.

## Deepening the Connection

One day, I got a call from one of my clients, Gabe, and he was frustrated because he had been getting dates left and right. I know, it seemed like a good problem to me too. I later found out that his dates would hit a wall and never lead to anything. He would literally run an interaction from A to Z, even sleep with the girl on a first date, but somehow wouldn't see them again.

My response to him was "that's your problem." It totally made sense to me and I showed him why.

He was good at building attraction because he had so much going for him. He was a successful businessman, had great looks, and had a lot to offer to the girl.

The problem was that he relied on these things and came off as a "fuckboy" that the girl didn't really have a deep connection with, but was attracted to.

He was extremely frustrated, but the answer was simple - vulnerability.

Gabe spent so much time and focus on getting the girls to talk about themselves, and showing them his lifestyle that he was never real with them. This is why the high value mindset isn't just about material and lifestyle, it's about who you are, and if you can't convey who you are to another person, then they will never know.

He was basically tired of being treated like a piece of meat and wanted something real, and this date he had coming up was with a girl he really liked and he didn't want to mess it up, so he called me to prepare.

I had to push his comfort zone to open him up. We talked for an hour about all the topics he never shared with people. I explained to him that the vulnerability he had just shown was a strength, not a weakness. The only time it becomes a weakness is when you feel pity for yourself and convey that to others, but when you have overcome or are working on overcoming the obstacles in your life or the things that hold you back, there is nothing more respectable.

Then we went over how and when to approach these topics on the date and where to take it from there. He ended up going on a second date with that girl, and a third, and a fourth. They've been together now for over three years.

# SECTION III

## THE HIGH VALUE MINDSET IN OTHER ASPECTS OF YOUR LIFE

# Chapter 10 | Body language - Positioning & Escalation

*"Body language and tone of voice - not words - are our most powerful assessment tools."*
**– Christopher Voss**

Experts agree that 70% - 93% of communication is nonverbal. The most famous study since the 1960's by Dr. Mehrabian concluded the following results:

55% - body language

38% - vocal

7% - verbal

Given this information, I hope you understand how important your body language is. This is one of the biggest reasons why most guys fail. As we talked about in earlier chapters, a girl will test how congruent you are in what you are saying and what your body is saying. This is why you can lie about your confidence to a girl to build attraction, but you can't sustain the misleading information for long. Some girls will pick up on it immediately, others will give it a chance and see through it over time. Even in a relationship, a girl will test you to see if you are still someone she can trust to feel safe with. If you give in to her tests, she will lose attraction and neither of you will understand why. Then one day, she will blame it on losing the love and the spark and not feeling it anymore. It will feel sudden to you, but it has been building up for months.

Body language is crucial especially when talking to a stranger for the first time. From the moment you enter their awareness (not even talk to them), they are collecting massive amounts of information about you based on your physical look, actions, and movements. You can read confidence in a man based on the way he walks, takes a sip of his drink, or looks at you. The signs are everywhere, and girls are more attuned to these signs than guys are. Their brain has a larger capacity for reading and interpreting physical cues because evolutionarily their survival has been dependent on it. They need to know that you are safe and trust that you can protect them whether through resources or physical capability.

It's no surprise that the greatest attraction trigger for women is status and survivability, which is much different from the attraction trigger for men who primarily seek fertility that is evident in a girl's physical composition.

One of my students on a bootcamp, Sam, was doing such a great job approaching women for the first time. He was a business owner, in amazing shape, and a great sense of style. Even though he had all of these things going for him, there were a few things he did that subconsciously "threatened" a girl's safety.

In one instance, I approached a group of girls and engaged them in conversation. I introduced one of my students into the group then brought the rest of the students in. Sam was hitting it off with one of the girls, but there were more guys than girls in the group and body language was going to make the difference between keeping and losing this interaction.

I literally moved each guy to a position that would make the girls more comfortable. When I got Sam I needed to move him to the opposite side, so instead of guiding him I got his attention while the other guys kept the girls engaged and explained the concept. The girls were feeling slightly on edge because of the positioning of the guys which made them feel overpowered psychologically. I explained to Sam that he needed to give the exit side of the positioning to the girl he was talking to in order to make them feel safe.

I couldn't move the girl to the exit side, but I could lead her there. I told Sam that the girl he was talking to needed comfort and for him to take a couple steps to the side. The moment he listened to me, the other girl immediately moved to the place Sam was standing originally on the exit side of the group circle.

Sam was blown away by how I was able to pick up signals from the girls while the students were talking to them. He went home understanding the power of body language and understanding cues. That night he met with one of the girls we had met during the day and she they spent the night together. It was safe to say, that weekend was not just educational, but a memorable experience.

Body language matters in more than just group environments or conversations. It impacts attraction from the moment a girl becomes aware of your presence and could make the difference between keeping or losing a conversation.

One of my students came to me with a problem that he had been facing for 7 months. Jacob was consistently out practicing approaching in the daytime but was not able to get one date.

This came as a surprise to me because he knew how to have a solid conversation and lead it forward. I didn't see how he was not able to get a solid interaction until I had him approach someone for me a couple of times. I learned that most of the girls he would approach would not stop to talk in the first place, and if they did, they would leave not long after stopping. What he was missing wasn't conversation skills, but body language.

That night we spent two hours running drills on how to approach, position, and kickstart a conversation so that he could continue on his own from there. After spending all that time getting rejection after rejection he was so discouraged that  this was his last effort to do something about it.

The next day I gave him a challenge. He was intimidated by stopping a girl walking in the opposite direction, so I decided to help him. I made him run up to girls that had passed him already and it was too late to stop.

He thought that was a crazy idea, "They've already passed by and they're far by now, you want me to stop them now?" he asked.

"Yes," I said.

He looked at me for a second, then took off running after the girl. I waited for him for a little while until I saw him coming back with his posture straight, his chest out, and a big smile on his face. That was officially his breakthrough.

The next person he approached, he went up so confidently as if he expected to be given attention, and a positive response, and had nothing to lose because he was there to give, not take. When he came in with this new belief, the girl read it off of him and responded accordingly. People will treat you how you expect to be treated, and girls will be first to read how you feel about yourself.

We transcended his belief that he can't stop a girl walking in the opposite direction, much less run up to her after she has passed and end up in a conversation with her.

After demonstrating the techniques and explaining to him each piece of how his body communicates and what is going through the girl's mind at each point, he was able to engage a girl and carry a conversation and lead it forward. By the end of the day together, he had already set up two dates after 7 months of getting blown out.

That's the difference your body language can make. Even if you're good at conversation, it won't buy you any time with the girl because you haven't established credibility, empathy, and rapport, which you only have a few seconds to do with someone who has never met you before. It's important to come off non-threatening, and open on first impression. The girl is wondering who you are and what you want from her because we live in a world where she could be getting approached by anyone and not everyone will have good intentions, so her guard will be up until she realizes you're not trying to get anything from her. However, to show her that you're cool, you have to first buy time with her and that can only work when your body language communicates the right things about you because she is subconsciously collecting millions of pieces of information about you in seconds that will add up to a feeling of intuition she gets towards you. We all work this way because we have developed this mechanism for survival. Our conscious brain is slower than our subconscious brain, which is why most people will allow their feelings to guide their decisions, even though feelings are not always correct.

To overcome this innate wall, you must convey a first impression with your body language before you have a chance to speak. Mastering this skill will help you tremendously in approaching strangers and making people feel connected to you.

## Giving Away Your Power Through Body Language

Let's talk about the subtle power plays in our interactions, especially when we're trying to connect with someone. It's like a silent conversation that's always happening, whether we're aware of it or not. And in the realm of dating, getting this silent convo right can mean the difference between sparking interest and coming off as needy. Here are the most common things to watch out for throughout your entire interaction.

### The Lean-In

Ever found yourself leaning in too much when talking to someone you're interested in? It might be to catch what they're saying or make sure they hear you. But here's the thing: if they really want to hear you, they'll lean in too. Leaning in too much can actually send a message that you're trying a bit too hard. If you notice you're doing all the leaning, it might be a sign to dial it back a notch.

### Giving and Getting Space

Now, instead of invading personal space, try this: give space and use your own. Make yourself open and inviting, but don't crowd them. And sometimes, turn away a bit. It shows you're not clinging on to every word and you're confident enough to give them room. This dance of closeness and space speaks volumes. It says, "I'm interested, but I'm also cool doing my own thing."

### Reading the Room

Paying attention to their body language is just as important. Are they mirroring your openness or are they more closed off? If you're getting signals that they're not really into the conversation, it might be your cue to gracefully exit stage left. Showing that you're okay walking away first is a strong move. It shows you're not desperate for their attention.

### Try-Hard vs. Laid-Back

Being too eager can backfire. You know the type: nodding too much, sticking too close, or mirroring every single move. It screams, "I need your approval." What works better is a laid-back approach. Stay engaged, but comfortable. Show interest without the pressure. It's about finding that sweet spot where you're interested but not hanging on their every word.

So, when it comes to body language, think of it as your silent wingman. Use it wisely to show confidence and interest without crossing into neediness. It's all about that balance.

# CHAPTER 11 | Elevating Your Lifestyle

*"People are drawn to shared interests, shared problems, and an individual's life energy... Humans connect with humans. Hiding one's humanity and trying to project an image of perfection makes a person vague, slippery, lifeless, and uninteresting."*
*— Robert Glover, No More Mr. Nice Guy*

In the journey to becoming a high-value individual that attracts the right people into your life, you've already taken significant steps. You've learned to create or find the right environments and mastered the art of leading conversations. Now, it's time to delve into the third step, a step that can truly transform your life - elevating your lifestyle.

Imagine Mark. Mark is the quintessential high-value man - successful, ambitious, and charismatic. But there's something unique about Mark. He lives his life to the fullest. Every day, he's out and about, engaging in activities he's passionate about, and creating opportunities for meaningful interactions. Mark is the type of person others naturally gravitate towards.

In reality, Mark is a friend of mine and this is the story of how he changed his life once he made the decision to. Mark was a successful man in his early thirties, but was once like many others, stuck in the daily grind. Work consumed most of his time, and he often found himself isolated, wondering why he couldn't forge meaningful connections. Then, one day, he decided to make a change.

## The Power of Social Circles

Mark realized that to attract high-value people into his life, he needed to be passionate about something other than work. He took up hiking, a hobby he had always been curious about but never pursued. As he explored new trails and conquered challenging peaks, he not only found joy but also met like-minded individuals who shared his love for the outdoors. Typically, people who wake up at 6 a.m. and take care of their physical health, are disciplined in other ways in life. So, this was a proper outlet to meet people that would add more to his life other than just as exercise partners. This is where his social circle started to grow, as he decided to embrace the fact that these things will always be top priority and life will never accommodate his goals.

Mark's newfound passion for hiking led to an idea - he could organize hiking trips and invite others to join. These outings weren't just about the hike; they were about building connections. Mark's friends began bringing their friends, and soon, the hiking group became a close-knit community. I myself joined several hikes, and even ended up making close connections with a few people that I invited to my own events. Mark's social circle was growing organically, and he was creating a social hub.

Not only did Mark have a solid group of people to hike with, but now they were friends, and they decided to go even bigger with their idea for a hiking group. They decided to expand the group to the public and start raising money to help families in need through their hiking adventures.

More and more people started joining to support their cause because it resonated with them. Soon people would just come to the hikes because they loved the community that Mike and his friends had built. On top of that, people looked up to Mike as the leader because it was his creation. His status in the group he had created was also an attractive quality and with him meeting so many people regularly, he would meet a lot of women that he had the opportunity to get to know as they loved joining the hikes and meeting people as well.

People would bring their dogs and socialize. Eventually Mark and his friends decided to go all out and start a non-profit. They expanded this idea to start hosting fundraising events outside of hiking. They started throwing holiday parties, photoshoots, and coordinating with other nonprofits to collaborate together. They even got the city involved to rent out an entire park and bring vendors to bring 700 people together and $10k raise.

Mark didn't start out thinking that he was going to end up bringing so many people together. He started out from a simple decision to pursue things that give him joy and build a life for himself that he is happy with. The key to Mark's success wasn't just about having events; it was about exuding genuine joy. He wasn't doing it to impress anyone; he was doing it because he loved it, and he understood that any level of change is going to start from himself. His enthusiasm was infectious, drawing others into his orbit because he was focused on being a man of value in order to give value to others. People didn't just want to be around Mark; they wanted to be like him.

## Fueling Your Daily Joy

Elevating your lifestyle isn't limited to grand events or extravagant outings; it starts with finding joy in your daily life. Here are some tips to help you on this journey:

Just like Mark, discover what truly excites you. It could be hiking, painting, playing music, or anything that sparks your interest. When you're passionate about something, your enthusiasm becomes magnetic.

Once you do a little exploration into what lights your soul on fire, don't keep that passion to yourself. Find a way to make the thing you're passionate about, more social and active. Invite others to join you in your activities. It could be a weekly game night, a cooking class, or even a book club. Shared experiences create lasting bonds.

If there aren't events or groups that align with your interests, take the initiative to create them. Host gatherings or activities that reflect your passions, and watch your social circle expand.

Growth often happens outside your comfort zone. Be open to meeting new people and trying new things. Embrace the unknown, and you'll be rewarded with new experiences and connections.

One common mistake people make is confining themselves to their homes. In today's digital age, it's easy to fall into the trap of virtual connections. While online interactions have their place, there's no substitute for real-life experiences.

As we covered in the first step of the framework, getting out of the house exposes you to diverse environments, cultures, and perspectives. It encourages face-to-face interactions, which are richer and more meaningful. High-value individuals understand the importance of being physically present in the world and actively participating in it.

Moreover, being out of the house fosters a sense of adventure. It's where you stumble upon unexpected opportunities and serendipitous encounters. These are the moments that can change the course of your life.

Elevating your lifestyle is not just about attracting the right people; it's about living a fulfilled and purpose-driven life. Mark's story serves as a powerful example of how embracing your passions, creating genuine connections, and living authentically can transform your social life and overall well-being.

So, as you embark on this journey, remember that the path to becoming a high-value individual isn't just about reaching a destination; it's about savoring the journey itself. Embrace your passions, create meaningful experiences, and let the joy of living guide you. In doing so, you'll not only attract the right people but also become the kind of person others aspire to be and be around.

# CHAPTER 12 | The High Value Mindset and Wealth

*"More money does not solve money problems. Different relationships do not solve relationship problems... Money does not make you good with money. Love does not make you love yourself. Relationships don't make you good at relationships. Work does not make you good at your job or capable of work life balance. Problems don't inherently make you a stronger person unless you change and adapt. The variable is you. The common denominator is whether or not you shift your foundational perspective on the world and how you behave within it. Someone who makes $500k can be as seriously in debt and struggling as someone who makes $50k. And in fact, this happens more often than you think."*
— ***Brianna Wiest*, The Mountain is You**

I will start off by saying money is important in our modern society, but money does not define wealth. The amount of money you have only defines how rich you are and even that is subjective. Riches on their own will not make you fulfilled. I know plenty borderline suicidal rich (or what people consider rich) people getting therapy and mentorship for the problems they have in their personal lives because a dollar amount is just one small factor in the grand scheme of your life.

Wealth, at its very depth, is a belief in yourself. Not just confidence, but borderline delusion. I don't believe in delusion because there's so much that affects us and our lives that is beyond the human capacity to see or understand. I believe it's very reasonable to fully believe you can win while having every logical justification as to why you can't, because besides the reasoning and rationale that leads you to believe something about yourself, the belief itself is powerful no matter what it's based on. Feel it, believe it, act like it.

Where does this level of confidence and drive come from? Staying true to your deepest most authentic self - your self respect, your self compassion, your self love, your self forgiveness, and most importantly, your authentic self expression. Wealth and prosperity find their roots in living life on your terms, whether that means freedom of time or freedom of location to be wherever you want to be. It's not uncommon to find individuals earning six figures but living paycheck to paycheck. The disparity between financial success and true wealth becomes evident when one is not aligned with their values and purpose.

So, what does that delusional confidence look like and where does it lead to? Becoming the king of your domain, gaining the freedom to roam as you please, and being able to include and incorporate anyone you choose into your new way of life. You will not only feel energized every day, but you will also be the ruler of your space, not just physically, but energetically. This requires effort and relative risk taking on your part because it involves putting yourself out there and taking responsibility for everything in your life, but this is the only way you will be fulfilled, not by sitting in comfort and waiting for someone to heal you and take action for you.

Wealth also comes in the form of gratitude. It's having a thousand dollars in the bank, and knowing you're rich. Not by staring in the mirror and repeating affirmations to yourself, but by being grateful that you have a thousand dollars in the bank where others are going bankrupt, or losing family members to disease. It's having the potential to earn millions and the purpose to serve others or a mission beyond yourself.

True wealth is not confined to a specific dollar amount; it transcends numerical values. Whether you have a thousand or a million in the bank, your wealth is determined by what you value and the goals you pursue. The amount becomes irrelevant; it's the mindset that defines richness or poverty.

Comparisons often distort our perception of wealth. A "rich" person might feel poor compared to Elon Musk and a "poor" person might feel rich compared to Gandhi in the second half of his life, but Gandhi felt more rich and fulfilled than many, even more so after leaving his profession as a lawyer because he had a purpose he served bigger than himself.

The realization that wealth is relative highlights the importance of defining it on a personal level. Rich people can experience depression and feelings of inadequacy at any level, emphasizing that true wealth goes beyond monetary success.

Wealth can be categorized in four ways: Financial wealth, social wealth, time wealth, and health wealth.

## Financial Wealth

This is the most commonly recognized type of wealth and involves the accumulation of money and assets. It includes income, savings, investments, and any material possessions that contribute to one's financial security.

## Social Wealth

Social wealth pertains to the quality and depth of your relationships and social connections. It includes friendships, family bonds, professional networks, and the overall support system you have in your life.

## Time Wealth

Time is a valuable resource, and time wealth focuses on how effectively you manage and utilize your time. It's about having the freedom to spend time on activities that bring fulfillment, joy, and personal development.

## Health Wealth

Health wealth is concerned with your physical and mental well-being. It encompasses factors such as fitness, nutrition, mental health, and overall lifestyle choices that contribute to a healthy and balanced life.

I knew a man named Alex who embarked on a journey to transform his life and embody the essence of true wealth. He understood that attracting genuine connections begins with cultivating different dimensions of wealth within oneself.

Alex recognized the importance of financial stability, not just for external success but as a means to create a life of abundance as a high value man. He worked diligently on his career, invested wisely, and managed his finances responsibly. This financial discipline allowed him to pursue his passions and contribute meaningfully to others.

In his quest for holistic well-being, Alex valued his relationships deeply. He invested time and effort into building strong connections with friends, family, and his community. His genuine interest in others and willingness to support them created a network of trust and reciprocity that enriched his life.

Understanding that time is a precious resource, Alex sought balance. He learned to prioritize activities that aligned with his values, passions, and personal growth. By managing his time effectively, he created space for self-reflection, learning, and pursuing endeavors that brought him joy and fulfillment.

Recognizing the importance of physical and mental well-being, Alex prioritized his health. He embraced a lifestyle that included regular exercise, a balanced diet, and mindfulness practices. This not only improved his physical vitality but also enhanced his mental clarity and emotional resilience.

As Alex continued on his journey, he realized that the foundation of all these forms of wealth was his relationship with himself. Being self-aware, he embraced authenticity, love, and gratitude as guiding principles in his life.

Alex approached life with a heart full of love and gratitude. He appreciated the beauty in everyday moments, expressed gratitude for his relationships, and radiated a positive energy that attracted others toward him.

In the end, Alex's journey was not just about attracting romantic relationships but about creating a life rich in meaningful connections, purpose, and fulfillment. His story serves as a reminder that true wealth begins within, and by nurturing oneself with authenticity, love, and gratitude, one can attract and contribute to the abundance of life.

All of these forms of wealth allude to your relationship with yourself and your level of self-awareness, love, and gratitude. What this looks like in each form is that you have the drive to pursue your career because you believe in yourself. You value relationships and add value to others' lives by being a source of value yourself. You prioritize and value your time and have the freedom to pursue things that make you happy. Lastly, you take care of yourself physically, mentally, and emotionally, not out of self-hate or punishment to put yourself through hardship for growth, but out of self-love knowing that you deserve to be better without having an expectation of where you should be. If you don't have a good relationship with yourself you won't be happy with anyone else and you'll ultimately have difficulty keeping people around.

# CHAPTER 13 | Wealth's Impact on Attraction

*"Abundance is scooped from abundance yet abundance remains."*
*– Anne Sexton*

Now for the part you've been waiting for.

In the realm of dating and self-development, the concept of wealth again goes far beyond the digits in your bank account. It's not just about financial prosperity but a holistic approach to living a fulfilled life. Let's delve into the mindset that defines true wealth and its profound impact on attraction.

Several years ago I was dating a model who was a few years older than me. At the time I didn't have much material wealth. I was driving an old Lexus with nothing but a cassette player. I had to use those converters that have an AUX cable attached to the cassette so I could play music from my phone. All I had to offer her was an emotional connection and my energy, and this is an example of how powerful that can be.

Not only was she against dating someone younger than her, but she had guys left and right trying to take her out. When we met we had a deep connection, but her stigma on age was holding her back from seeing me again. It took some calibrated persistence to get her out on one date and she didn't have to see me again after that.

When we finally went out I made no moves on her and I didn't have a car so I would have to ask my friends for a ride home that day. Later she told me that when I had the opportunity to kiss her that day, but didn't, she felt really attracted and impressed.

At the end of the first date, she offered to take me home, and when we got home I told her that if she doesn't want to see me again that she can delete my number from her phone and my phone. She refused, and the rest was history.

Every time we went out she would see me making friends everywhere we'd go. She would go to the bathroom and come back to me knowing the workers by name and introducing her to two or three other girls within the time that she was in the bathroom. She saw that I had options too and it built comfort in her to know that I don't need her.

After a few dates I got a glimpse into her life. She would tell me about the guys reaching out to her and wanting to meet. One time she flaked on plans with a guy she knew that was coming to pick her up in his Ferrari, to stay home with me and watch a movie. That was when I understood the power of giving a girl an emotional experience.

She wasn't attracted to the things I had, she was attracted to my energy, my abundant mindset, and my potential and sense of purpose. She knew a lot about me in a short period of time. She saw that I was socially aware, had leadership qualities, and big dreams to accomplish. I knew the same things about her, and from her perspective, she had a safe space to express her deeper self with me. When a girl can say she was part of your come-up story, it's a bigger flex than her telling her friends that she's dating a rich guy with no social skills.

One of my mentors met his now wife at a time when he was going bankrupt on his businesses and had no money. At the same time she was making six figures. Now he's a millionaire and people often judge that she is with him for the money not knowing that she would pay for their dates when they had just started dating.

The story of my mentor, whose wife financially supported their early relationship, is a testament to the power of ambition and goals. What drew her in was not the size of his paycheck but the fire in his belly, the drive to achieve something greater. It's the focused and ambitious mindset that creates magnetic attraction.

In the world of dating, potential and purpose far outweigh the allure of a fat wallet. The concept of submitting to the mission, embracing a purpose-driven life, becomes the cornerstone of true wealth. It's not about the dollar amount you bring to the table; it's about the mindset and attitude of being wealth-oriented.

What you lack in emotional connection you will have to make up for with material. If you need material to entice a girl to spend time with you, that's a clear sign you're on the wrong path.

Wealth is not just a mindset. Wealth is a way of life. You don't just get wealth, you become wealthy. And you don't just become wealthy, you choose to accept it and live it, you open yourself up to it. Your potential is more important than your pockets, and relationships and respect are the building blocks. Money only amplifies what you build in yourself because it gives you a wider range of expression. True wealth is living a life aligned with your values and pursuing goals that fulfill you. Understanding that money is a tool to amplify character, not redefine it, forms the essence of holistic success in wealth.

# CHAPTER 14 | Mentors

*"Old men are always advising young men to save money. That is bad advice. Don't save every nickel. Invest in yourself. I never saved a dollar until I was forty years old."*
**– Henry Ford**

Let's build out a hypothetical scenario.

You get on this journey of becoming the best version of yourself, and being the person that women want to have and men want to be. You understand you have to put the work in and believe that you're capable and worthy so you start making time to socialize and meet new people.

You end up meeting a girl that makes you feel alive. She is undeniably beautiful, with a mysterious allure that draws you in like a moth to a flame. She has an air of sophistication and charisma that makes her stand out from the other girls.

It turns out you have a lot in common and you connect with her well. You start dating and having fun together. You love spending time with her, it's addicting, you wake up and go to sleep thinking about her.

You find yourself craving her attention and always checking your phone to see if she texted you. When you go on dates, you feel like you won her over again every time you impress her. You take her to nice places and buy her nice things to make her happy and she loves you for it.

When she's sad, she calls you and you try to be there for her to comfort her and tell her everything is okay. When she has a problem you listen to her and try to fix it for her. She tells you a lot about her ex who mistreated her and you agree that he's an asshole in attempts to be supportive, not taking the time to question her and dig deeper.

When she lets you kiss her you feel rewarded for your efforts. Every time you kiss her it feels like a victory and you get excited. You've tried to have sex with her, but she always pulls back without explanation. One time she mentioned that she's still getting over her ex and is not ready to have sex.

You've been on several dates already, but some days she doesn't text you back all day and other days she says she already has plans and can't hang out. You don't take it as a big deal and continue pursuing this girl because you have feelings for her. You're always checking up on her to make sure she's ok because she seems to be sad quite often and that's unfortunate.

After dating for a month, you finally have sex and it's amazing. Each time it just keeps getting better. As dating progresses she starts wanting a relationship, but you want to take your time getting to know her. On the other hand she wants reassurance that you're not just using her. You want to give it time to see how she fits into your life but you decide to go ahead and have the conversation for the sake of her feeling better about it.

After some time you start noticing that she doesn't listen to you as much as she used to or respect what you have to say. You start having arguments that end in frustration and never get resolved. On the other hand, there's a lot of romance between you. She seems to know how to push your buttons in good ways and bad.

You start noticing her attention going away when you're on dates. She'll be on her phone a lot while you're talking even though you told her it bothers you and when you go out she will flirt back with guys that approach her. When you get mad at her she says "He was being nice" and "It was just a conversation."

One day she will be very loving towards you, another day she will blame you for little things. Her mood swings and demands often leave you feeling drained and emotionally battered. She makes you feel responsible for her happiness, and you go to great lengths to please her because she is your girlfriend, but it feels like the more you do the less she does for you.

The sex is amazing and just keeps getting better. She tells you she wants kids and you decide to marry her because you've built a whole relationship with her and that's the natural next step. She wants a new house so you take your savings and invest in a new home a little earlier than you planned. You're living check to check and having trouble keeping up with her demands.

One day you come home and she tells you she doesn't love you anymore. You ask her why and she responds that she hasn't felt "butterflies" for a long time now. You don't know what to do with yourself. You try to convince her but it pushes her away even more. She files for divorce, you lose the house and half your assets because you ended up in a relationship with a manipulative person who was avoidant and once the relationship became comfortable, she started lacking the anxious attachment which she associated with true love.

Because you did not take the time to understand yourself, heal, and in turn understand others, you did not see these signs coming, even before the relationship. You hadn't gotten to know enough people and done the work on yourself to develop your emotional intelligence, or EQ, enough to recognize people and understand their attachments. Then you hire a coach because you don't want to repeat that life lesson and lose everything again.

That EQ is the most important part of learning social skills, and it not only helps you with women, but it's a transferable skill that will benefit you with making money, getting a raise, negotiating deals, and making friends.

If you're trying to become a firefighter, would you want to be taught how to handle fires correctly and have protective gear while doing it? It would be a good idea. A coach is your protective gear and guidance. Having someone there for you watching every move in the social world and giving you proper explanations is going to make the difference between suffering the rest of your life and mastering your domain. It will teach you about keeping the right people around you, establishing boundaries, spotting toxic qualities, and learning how to better understand, manage, and influence your own emotions as well as others'. Doing all of that on your own, is going to take a while, and you only have so much life to live.

You had been putting money before your happiness and you finally decided to put happiness and growth before money because you are your greatest asset that no one can take away. Now you have a better social life and better job because you took initiative and started digging deep into why you were getting the results that you were. As you become more aligned with the person you want to be, your life adjusts to meet your expectations and your scarcity mindset doesn't have power over you.

Know that you can level up by yourself, but you cannot reach your full potential, and it will take much longer to do it.

As you work on yourself you will need the help of people around you to guide you and foster this new identity.

One of my favorite quotes by Sir Isaac Newton says "If I have seen further, it is by standing on the shoulders of giants." Newton didn't invent calculus out of thin air. He took from the ideas of Gottfried Liebniz and was influenced by many others. The greatest artists do not reinvent art, they build on the ideas of great artists.

There are three main qualifiers to consider in choosing a mentor to work with.

## 1. Authority & Credibility

If you take nothing else from this chapter, take this piece of advice - work with someone who has already gotten the results that you want. If you want to make a million dollars, learn from someone who has made a million dollars.

One of the biggest green flags for me with coaches, is when your coach has coaches of his own. I am more willing to invest in someone who continues to invest in himself. Most of the coaches I have had in my life have had coaches of their own and I have learned not only from them, but the knowledge they learn also gets passed down to me.

## 2. Passion & Commitment

This is a two way street. Before you work with anyone, you must first decide if you are committed to your growth and ready to go all in, or if you're just interested in learning. If you're just interested, read books, but if you're sick and tired of being sick and tired and ready to go all in, then work with a coach and choose one that matches that energy. Your coach must be committed to your growth as much as you are.

If your coach is not passionate about the subject, they will not be committed to your growth. If your coach doesn't seem committed about the results you get, they are not going to change. It's like getting into a relationship and ignoring red flags hoping you can overcome them and change the person you're with. Most likely, the person is not going to change unless they are aware and actively working on themselves to change. Otherwise, you will not convince them.

## 3. Ethics & Values

If you meet a coach that will take money from anyone without first knowing that he can help them, then you should reconsider working with that person.

There are countless coaches out there that build an entire business on marketing and collect a cult following to exploit and make money off of without considering how the person will be affected.

Honesty is one of the most important traits in a relationship, whether it's a friend, a business partner, or a coach. The values he has will massively influence the way you learn, whether it's putting the time in to make sure you understand something or serving as an example for you to emulate.

After a year of working on my business I had finally started profiting. I had collected $10,200 and I spent $7,000 on a coach. After a year of working, the moment I had enough money I invested it in my growth.

Instead of working another year for another $10,000, I made $15,000 the following month. In the same way, instead of spending another year approaching girls, doing and saying the same things, you can jump leagues ahead by paying someone who sees the things you don't see.

Contrary to popular belief, volume does not equate to growth. Practicing doing the wrong things and having some success thinking you're doing it right and you continue solidifying those habits and not knowing why some people react the way they do with you but you don't care enough because you are getting some of the results that you want, which keeps you comfortably ignorant.

## The Right Coach

When you find the right coach they will become your best friend because development in yourself, your business and relationships all revolve around who you are and you need someone that is willing to take on the task of entering your life, deconstructing the things that are hurting you, and building you up as a different person and the resistance that will come with your old sense of identity fighting back against change.

I've had students tell me "I'm so glad I found you" when they were about to give up on themselves where all that was missing was a slight shift in approach and conversation. Others have had worse starting points where they had never approached a stranger much less learned to connect with them and we had to deconstruct the underlying fears down to the core beliefs that were feeding them. It takes a special type of person to be able to commit to your growth to the extent of digging deeper into the things in your life and mindset that are holding you back, not just in talking to women but in embracing your full authenticity and leveling up so that you know how to be liked and respected in any situation where most people would be passive and indifferent.

So here's a challenge for you if you choose to accept it. There are a lot of self help books and materials out there but if you don't do anything about it it becomes a shelf help book. So here's my challenge:

Reach out to me directly and let me know you read this and let's hop on a call to hear your insights and see how I can help you achieve your dreams.

If you're ready to be mentored, send me an email and let's have a conversation about what that would look like for you.

gslifestyleco@gmail.com

Go and conquer.

Speak to you soon!

Made in United States
Troutdale, OR
05/07/2024

19699925R00076